Professional Autonomy in Video Relay Service Interpreting

Studies in
Interpretation

Melanie Metzger and Earl Fleetwood, Editors

VOLUME 1 *From Topic Boundaries to Omission: New Research on Interpretation*

VOLUME 2 *Attitudes, Innuendo, and Regulators*

VOLUME 3 *Translation, Sociolinguistic, and Consumer Issues in Interpreting*

VOLUME 4 *Interpreting in Legal Settings*

VOLUME 5 *Prosodic Markers and Utterance Boundaries in American Sign Language Interpretation*

VOLUME 6 *Toward a Deaf Translation Norm*

VOLUME 7 *Interpreting in Multilingual, Multicultural Contexts*

VOLUME 8 *Video Relay Service Interpreters*

VOLUME 9 *Signed Language Interpreting in Brazil*

VOLUME 10 *More Than Meets the Eye*

VOLUME 11 *Deaf Interpreters at Work*

VOLUME 12 *Investigations in Healthcare Interpreting*

VOLUME 13 *Signed Language Interpretation and Translation Research*

VOLUME 14 *Linguistic Coping Strategies in Sign Language Interpreting*

VOLUME 15 *Signed Language Interpreting in the Workplace*

VOLUME 16 *Here or There*

VOLUME 17 *Professional Autonomy in Video Relay Service Interpreting*

Professional Autonomy in Video Relay Service Interpreting

Erica Alley

GALLAUDET UNIVERSITY PRESS
Washington, DC

Studies in Interpretation
A Series Edited by Melanie Metzger and Earl Fleetwood

Gallaudet University Press
Washington, DC 20002
http://gupress.gallaudet.edu

ISBN 978-1-944838-45-4
ISSN 1545-7613

∞ This paper meets the requirements of ANSI/NISO Z39.48-1992 (Permanence of Paper).

Front and back cover image by Paul Klee (1879–1940). © 2019 Artists Rights Society (ARS), New York. *Static-Dynamic Gradation,* 1923. Oil and gouache on paper, bordered with gouache, watercolor, and ink, 15 x 10.25 in. (38.1 x 26.1 cm.). The Berggruen Klee Collection, 1987 (1987.455.12). The Metropolitan Museum of Art, New York, NY, USA. Photo Credit: Image copyright © The Metropolitan Museum of Art. Image source: Art Resource, NY. Reproduced with permission.

Cover design by Katie Lee.

Contents

Preface   vii

CHAPTER 1. Professions and Society   1

CHAPTER 2. Professional Autonomy and Video Relay Service   21

CHAPTER 3. Provider Tracking of Communications
Assistant Work   43

CHAPTER 4. Providing Customer Service   76

CHAPTER 5. Lessons From the Past Inform the Future   95

Appendix A. A History of Telecommunications:
From Telegraph to Video Relay Service   101

Appendix B. Methods and Procedures   104

Appendix C. Interview Script   113

Appendix D. Additional Questions Posed by Interviewer   114

References   117

Index   127

Preface

In 2007, video relay service (VRS) was a fairly new enterprise in the signed language interpreting profession. I was then a novice American Sign Language (ASL)–English interpreter enrolled in a graduate program in interpreting. Like many of my fellow students, I was eager to cut my teeth on this new service, intrigued with the idea of providing interpretations via video technology. Upon being hired by a VRS provider, I was given the title of communications assistant (CA), along with the promise of an opportunity to be mentored within the company's training program. It appeared to be the perfect way for me to be safely inducted into the interpreting profession.

However, during my first week of work, I immediately felt uncomfortable with one of the instructions given to me by the VRS company manager. He explained that I might occasionally receive calls from deaf consumers who would ask to be connected to podcasts (lengthy noninteractive audio recordings about a variety of topics). He stated that some of the deaf callers might instruct me to not interpret the podcast and that I should honor their request but remain on line for the duration of the podcast, despite its length. These types of calls were even given a special name—"r-calls" or "rest calls"—creating the impression that these calls were a perk for the interpreter. Even as a novice interpreter, I felt there was something odd about this arrangement, but when I questioned my manager, he told me that r-calls were a common practice among VRS providers and they were handled in this manner because of "the need for emerging companies to succeed in the industry as they competed with larger VRS providers." The explanation seemed implausible, but as a new CA in VRS and as a novice interpreter, I uncomfortably accepted his explanations. However, I was in a quandary about how to address these r-calls: if I refused to accept them, I might have been perceived as being insubordinate and could possibly lose my job, but if I accepted the so-called r-calls without interpreting them, I felt I was deviating from ethical interpreting practice. Wasn't the goal of my work to convey an equivalent message between communicative participants? After a few weeks, my distrust grew of both this situation and the company, and I decided to leave my position.

This experience left me wondering about the rules that govern the work of CAs[1] in the VRS setting. Personally, I was unable to identify whether rules originated with the Federal Communications Commission (FCC) or individual VRS companies. I wondered if other CAs were aware of the origin of the rules that govern their work. To pursue these questions, I conducted a small-scale investigation into the origin and nature of rules in VRS. Using a semistructured interview protocol, I interviewed four interpreters who worked as either CAs or held leadership roles in the VRS industry (Alley, 2014). The results of this pilot study revealed that although interpreters were aware of the rules governing their work in VRS, they were often uncertain about the purpose of the rules or who was responsible for the establishment of the rules. The question of responsibility was evident as participants repeatedly discussed the roles and responsibilities of the following three parties in establishing VRS rules and guidelines: (a) the national organization of signed language interpreters, the Registry of Interpreters for the Deaf (RID), in developing a Standard Practice Paper; (b) interpreter education programs in preparing students for VRS work; and (c) FCC as the legal backbone of VRS rules and how that oversight drove VRS providers to create additional rules.

The theme of responsibility recurred when participants discussed their own VRS work. Participants stated they felt they had a responsibility to produce quality interpretations and provide excellent customer service for VRS consumers. According to the participants, supervisors focused on the statistical data presented in reports to both meet FCC requirements and produce billable minutes. Although it was clear that many players were involved in the VRS conglomerate, participants exhibited uncertainty about who was responsible for the various constraints that influ-

---

1. For the purpose of clarity, I distinguish the usage of the terms *communications assistant (CA)* and *interpreter* throughout this text. From a bureaucratic standpoint (i.e., Federal Communications Commission and individual VRS providers), individuals who provide ASL–English interpretation in the VRS environment are communications assistants; therefore, when discussing the work performed by these individuals from an organizational standpoint, I use the term *communications assistants* or *CAs*. However, the participants in this study most often refer to themselves as interpreters, which reflects their self-perception and the work that they perform in VRS. Throughout this text, I will follow the preferred term of either the VRS provider or the participant.

enced VRS work. One participant, a leader in the RID Video Interpreters Members Section (VIMS), described the dynamics as follows:

> I think the FCC is upset at the providers and the providers are upset with the FCC, and . . . the interpreters are standing in the middle. . . . The providers saying, "Well you have to do this or you're gonna lose your job." So then everyone goes into a panic and, "Omigod, the FCC's gonna take our job away!" No the FCC's not, your provider's not gonna pay you. . . . And the interpreter is standing in the middle [trying to understand whose fault it is], "Well is it the FCC or is it my provider?" Who do I need to be looking at to be asking for something? And, more often than not, interpreters are starting to look at RID [who's saying], "We're doing everything we can and we're on the same page as the FCC here. The problem is with the providers."

This quote suggests that CAs are aware that governing bodies constrain their work in VRS but are unclear regarding which organization (i.e., FCC or individual provider) sets the controls in their work. Providers may be placing blame on the FCC's regulatory practices, suggesting that the FCC makes providers closely regulate CA work. In reality, many rules that govern the work of CAs are provider initiated. The participant quoted also described an attempt of the VIMS to approach the FCC with its concerns. She described the FCC's response as follows:

> If it doesn't directly affect customer service the FCC won't make any regulations on it. So at some point interpreters wanted the FCC to make a requirement saying [interpreters] couldn't work over a percentage of billable time to make sure that interpreters don't get injured. Well, they came back and said "Well, that's an employee relation issue. We don't regulate that. That's under a whole different department in the federal government. You've got to go over to the labor org and talk to them. Don't talk to us."

So although the FCC is an authority regulating the provision of VRS, the FCC does not hold sway over aspects of CA work that involve employee relations (e.g., break time, shift selection, team interpreting). Although some providers assert that rules are established to adhere to FCC regulations, fraudulent activity within the VRS industry revealed that at least some VRS corporate rules were motivated by capitalist, profit-driven motives rather than long-established codes of ethical behavior.

Not long after leaving my position with VRS, I learned that the owner of the VRS provider I had worked for and several other VRS providers were under federal investigation for fraud. The r-calls I was instructed to accept were nothing more than a scheme intended to defraud the federal government of millions of dollars by billing the FCC for interpreting hours that never took place. The Department of Justice reported that the FCC reimbursed VRS corporate providers for these fraudulent claims at the rate of $390 per hour, for a total of tens of millions of dollars (U.S. Department of Justice, 2009). As a result of the investigation, 26 VRS owners and employees across the United States were indicted and convicted of felonies for their role in making (or causing others to make) fraudulent VRS calls and billing the government for those calls (U.S. Department of Justice, 2009).

Many interpreters who worked for the indicted VRS providers were not charged with crimes, but their reputations were tainted by their association with the companies. Some reported that they struggled to find positions with other VRS providers as the result of having been implicated in the scandal (personal communications, 2008). If I had continued to work for the VRS company, I would have unknowingly been complicit in fraudulent and illegal business practices and possibly suffered similar consequences. This experience opened my eyes to the serious problems that could arise with VRS guidelines and how interpreters view their own professional autonomy in VRS work. This motivated me to further explore the decisions VRS interpreters make in their work, within the construct of professional autonomy.

Because the four people that I originally spoke with were leaders in the VRS field (e.g., managers of VRS centers, VIMS board members) and were unsure of the origin of as well as the purpose behind the VRS rules, I wondered if they adhered to the rules. If not, how and when did they deviate from the rules? Did the interpreters in my pilot study represent the larger interpreting community in their understanding of work in VRS? The study described in this book aimed to examine the factors influencing decision making among VRS interpreters and the ways interpreters exercise professional autonomy in the VRS setting. To operationalize the construct of professional autonomy, I combined definitions of professional autonomy offered by Kasher (2005) and Sandstrom (2007) as (a) the ability to use reason and ethics to guide one's own actions, and (b) the freedom granted by the professional community and society to make decisions and act in a particular manner.

Naturally, examining professional autonomy leads to an investigation of the system under which interpreting takes place. Interpreting services are provided in systems that govern the actions of its participants. In line with this theory, the decisions made by a staff interpreter in a K–12 educational setting would align with the policies of the school where they are employed. The decisions of an interpreter in a hospital would follow protocols outlined by the hospital where they offer services. In this same vein, one could predict that the decisions made by an interpreter in VRS align with the rules that govern the VRS setting—those laid out by the provider as well as the FCC. Amid the confusion clearly felt by interpreters in VRS at the time of this study, further investigation is needed in order to gain understanding of the decision-making of interpreters in this environment.

Chapter 1

Professions and Society

Society does not perceive every occupation as having equal status (Wilensky, 1964). Rather, occupations are often characterized as being on a continuum (Greenwood, 1957) or a hierarchy (Liljegren, 2012). In this stratified approach, members of society generally do not perceive a truck driver as having the same status or prestige as a government official, or a plumber as having equal social standing as an engineer. Thus, the value that society places on a particular task shapes the perception that certain work is professional in nature. Other types of work may be regarded as legitimate and meaningful but are not awarded recognition as a profession.

The term *profession* has been examined and defined in a variety of ways (Abbott, 1988; Freidson, 1983). As early as the 1930s, sociologists studied professions in society, focusing on commonalities in the organization of professions and the characteristics of their members (Carr-Saunders & Wilson, 1933; Greenwood, 1957). Today, examinations of various aspects of professional life continue (Kasher, 2005). Professionals are typically described as possessing characteristics such as (a) having formal education from highly regarded institutions, (b) holding certification from a professional accrediting body, (c) adhering to a professional code of ethics, and (d) earning a living by performing the work full time (Abbott, 1988; Greenwood, 1957; Kasher, 2005). Professionals are seen as providing an intangible service (e.g., legal or medical advice) at the request of people who do not possess the specialized knowledge to perform a task independently and must trust another person's expertise (Macdonald, 1995; Rueschemeyer, 1983).

Abbott (1988) argues that examining professions based only on their structural aspects ignores a critical aspect of professions: the control that professionals have over the knowledge of their field and the ways in which they apply jurisdiction to their expertise. Krause (1996) suggests that the power held by members of a profession can be seen historically in the power held by guild masters. Guild masters controlled who could become a member, how new members were to be trained, and how they progressed from apprentice to journeyman to master craftsman. Although many craft guilds fell due to the growth of capitalism and the demand for speed and efficiency in product development, "economic and political factors allowed the scholars' guild and the guild model of the university to survive" (Krause, 1996, p. 10). These surviving guilds were a powerful force in producing medical, legal, and theological professionals.

According to Abbott (1988), the degree of power a worker holds demarcates a profession from an occupation. Power is awarded to individuals who have exclusive jurisdiction over the training of workers and provision of services, and this power is an indicator of the trust a community places in the professional (Greenwood, 1957; Macdonald, 1995; Wilensky, 1964). An example of this is the relationship between a client and his legal counsel, in which the client shares confidences that require a degree of trust in the professional. Similarly, the relationship between a patient and therapist indicates trust because the patient shares personal information with the belief that the therapist will not exploit or misuse the information (Rueschemeyer, 1983).

In an early study that foreshadowed a growing trend in American life, sociologist Greenwood (1957) writes, "Professional activity is coming to play a predominant role in the life patterns of increasing numbers of individuals of both sexes, occupying much of their waking moments, providing life goals, determining behavior, and shaping personality" (p. 45). Correspondingly, Goode (1957) characterizes professions as exclusive communities that exist within larger society. Goode (1957) writes that professions can be considered communities for the following reasons:

1. Its members are bound by a sense of identity.
2. Once in it, few leave, so that it is a terminal or continuing status for the most part.
3. Its members share values in common.
4. Its role definitions *vis-à-vis* both members and non-members are agreed upon and are the same for all members.
5. Within the areas of communal action there is common language, which is understood only partially by outsiders.
6. The community has power over its members.
7. Its limits are reasonably clear, though they are not physical and geographical, but social.
8. Though it does not produce the next generation biologically, it does so socially through its control over the selection of professional trainees, and through its training process it sends these recruits through an adult socialization process. (p. 194)

Characterizing professions as communities, of which only few people can become members, shows the social standing of professions and the power held by professionals.

Greenwood (1957) argues that occupations do not exist as binary categories (i.e., professional vs. nonprofessional), but are better conceptualized as being distributed along a continuum. At one end of the continuum are positions that clearly possess characteristics such as authority, skill, a theoretical foundation, and a culture. These positions are considered to have "community sanction" (p. 45). Greenwood suggests that the continuum allows for degrees of these characteristics as opposed to their unequivocal existence or lack thereof. Liljegren (2012) also agrees that professions are not binary, making the point that society often uses the metaphors of a hierarchy or a landscape to describe professions. According to Liljegren, the hierarchy is broken down into three layers: profession, semiprofession, and occupation, emphasizing society's perception of status within a particular field. In contrast, the landscape metaphor portrays professions in terms of boundaries, territories, gatekeeping, and social space. The reference that sociologists make regarding the power held by professions (Abbott, 1988; Macdonald, 1995; Wilensky, 1964) shows that specialized knowledge of the practitioner alone is not enough to characterize a profession, but rather society must recognize the complexity of the task and the skill of the practitioner. In addition, society must place its trust in the profession.

Indeed, the notions of trust and professionalism have historically been intertwined (Evetts, 2006). Society recognizes professionals as knowledgeable and trustworthy, which fosters social prestige associated with the work. According to many sociologists, when society assigns professional status to an occupation, it reduces personal control and enhances professional control (Abbott, 1988; Greenwood, 1957; Macdonald, 1995). However, society's positive view of professions is not without its skeptics. Some authors argue that members of society are increasingly suspicious of professions (Evetts, 2006). For example, Evetts (2006) notes that in a litigious society doctors are often accused of negligence or malpractice. Similarly, the promises made by government officials are frequently regarded as being dubious at best and are often considered self-serving. There is increasing acknowledgment in society that professionals can be motivated by either altruism (the desire to help others) or self-interest (the desire to help oneself), which influences the perception of professionals as being trustworthy (Flynn, 2009).

Many professionals work within large centralized systems that govern their work (Grint, 2005; Larson, 1980; Wilensky, 1964). Organizational systems include a hierarchy of offices, structured organizational procedures, and formal rules/regulations (Grint, 2005). The professional/ bureaucratic relationship is often described as one of conflict, even as these relationships are becoming the norm (Davies, 1983). Davies (1983) writes, "In the twentieth century, the concentration of corporate capital, the increased costs of professional preparation and of equipment and facilities, and the interventionist stance of the state are all factors which have effectively transformed the conditions under which professional work can be delivered" (p. 184). In current times, for example, doctors often do not practice independently, but instead work within the organization of a larger medical institution and are required to follow that institution's regulations. Similarly, lawyers must follow the rules of the law firm where they work. Bureaucracies evaluate success based on their ability to maximize profit and increase efficiency (Grint, 2005). Under this system, the professional who may take pride in her work is minimized to "routine rule following" (Davies, 1983, p. 177). In sum, the term *profession* carries with it a number of connotations (e.g., organizational structure, power, societal perception). Regardless of the lens used to explore professions, the notion of work changes drastically with the addition of technology.

TECHNOLOGY AND SOCIAL CHANGE

Technology has dramatically affected how workers understand and approach their work. In his early work, Karl Marx (1867/1976) advances the idea that technology initiates social change. Marx claims that the development of machines continuously changes the function of the worker. Similarly, the impact of technology on the worker can be seen in Eli Whitney's advancement of uniform interchangeable parts for the production of muskets in the early 1800s (Wren & Greenwood, 1999). Whitney's methods were designed to reduce the cost and time associated with customized production of each musket by individual workmen. The notion of interchangeable parts was quickly applied to the manufacturing of clocks, agricultural equipment, sewing machines, and other products of the time to foster expediency, exactness, and uniformity (Wren & Greenwood, 1999). Marx recognized that machines were invented and altered frequently to increase productivity and lower the cost of production. Workers with highly specialized skills were rendered obsolete after machines that could produce large quantities of products in less time were introduced. As a result, these specialized workers became the "disposable working population" (Marx, 1867/1976, p. 618).

Cowan (1976) investigated whether the technological change in household appliances had an effect on the American household. She points to innovations that replaced the laundry tub with the washing machine and the water pump with the sink faucet as having a major impact on the middle-class American household. She notes that technological advancements that affected tasks changed more than the work itself; they also changed the way society viewed the task. For example, after World War I, work such as laundry and cooking was no longer considered necessary, and society perceived this work as a sign of women's love for their family (Cowan, 1976).

Thirty years after Cowan's (1976) study (and 140 years after Marx's initial proclamation), Schneider (2006) argues that "technology, and change to it, are the dominant forces in society and in social change" (p. 91). Schneider defines technology as the material devices used by workers as well as the human capital required to implement the devices. For example, the machines used for product assembly (e.g., drilling, cutting), along with the workers who operate the machines, are considered cogs in the wheel of production. In addition, Schneider states that the introduction of machines and the need for machine operators led to the development of social structures, such as supervisors or managers on the production floor. The evolution of social structures can be seen as a type of technological determinism, which pinpoints change in technology as the most powerful instigator of social change (Chandler, n.d.).

In his seminal work, Postman (1992) suggests that, "A new technology does not add or subtract something. It changes everything" (p. 18). For example, Postman observed that the introduction of television into society led to its use in a variety of different venues for a number of reasons (e.g., education, politics, recreation). While Chandler (n.d.) warned that it is dangerous to consider technology the only cause of social change, it cannot be doubted that new technology initiates change. As Smith and Marx (1994) observe, anyone who has witnessed the development of the computer has seen how the advent of new technology can change the nature of daily life.

Applying this thinking, we may consider the ways in which the introduction of the videophone (i.e., technology) required communications assistants (CAs; i.e., human capital) to implement the videophone as a tool in society. The videophone and video relay service (VRS) provide deaf people access in ways that were not possible through original telephone technology. The technology of video streaming provided the breakthrough needed for deaf individuals to communicate using signed language with nonsigners via an interpreter (as well as directly with other signers) with a high degree of speed and efficiency. Every day, deaf people around the world rely on VRS to perform routine tasks such as checking in on a grandparent, ordering takeout food, or making appointments. Thus, the advent of video streaming technology, videophones, and VRS has resulted in access to telecommunication services that was not possible as recently as 25 years ago.

VRS has shifted interpreters' orientation from community-based practitioners to technology-based practitioners. As the result of this technological transition, Bailey (2005) observes, "The deaf community has become a sought after market niche discussed in boardrooms across the nation" (p. 15). To support VRS, thousands of signed language interpreters are employed to provide interpreting services 24 hours a day for calls between people using a signed language and people using a spoken language. VRS has also dramatically altered how thousands of American Sign Language (ASL)–English interpreters experience their professional lives. Although full-time positions are available for interpreters in some settings (e.g., education, government, medical), a large number of interpreters work as self-employed freelancers, which involves contracting for assignments based on the availability of the work and the discretion of the interpreter. Freelancing offers the benefit of flexible work schedules for interpreters, but lacks the security of a full-time position. For example, if an interpreter accepts an ongoing assignment in a postsecondary classroom but the Deaf student later withdraws from the course, the interpreter loses the guaranteed hours on which they were depending. Another limitation of freelancing is the limited opportunity for supervision and evaluation in the workplace. In some settings, employers do not have the skills to supervise or provide guidance to signed language interpreters. For example, this may be the case in a K–12 educational environment with a single deaf student or a business environment with a single deaf employee. In these settings, the system may not have a formal process to evaluate or support interpreters as well. As a result, freelance interpreters operate quite independently and experience a high degree of professional autonomy, allowing for independent decision making in their work.

Interpreting in VRS offers some of the benefits lacking in the freelance environment. A VRS Interpreting Task Analysis Report conducted by the Distance Opportunities for Interpreter Training Center (DO-IT Center) at the University of Northern Colorado found that interpreters are attracted to work in VRS as a result of the steady hours, consistent environment, professional wages, and corporate benefits (e.g., health insurance, retirement) (Johnson, Taylor, & Witter-Merithew, 2005). The report also states that VRS providers offer specialized training pertaining to VRS, which may serve as an additional incentive. However, as in other large-scale systems, such as hospitals or schools, employees are expected to manage their work within a tightly controlled environment, relinquishing the professional autonomy that they may have in other settings. As stated earlier, VRS providers must adhere to federal mandates established by the Federal Communications Commission (FCC). The FCC issues licenses to providers allowing them to conduct business and carefully monitors the provider-submitted reimbursement requests. The FCC mandates are translated into individual company policies; however, the policies instituted by individual VRS providers may reflect additional profit-focused motives that constrain the professional autonomy of CAs. For example, the FCC requires that 80% of VRS calls be answered within 120 seconds (FCC, n.d.). However, the FCC does not place constraints on the number of CAs working at any given point in time, nor does it stipulate the length of CA breaks during the day. Both of these conditions are developed by VRS providers, and both impact the ability of the provider to satisfy the FCC speed-of-answer requirement. Much like the interchangeable parts used in Whitney's production of muskets in the early 1800s (Wren & Greenwood, 1999), VRS providers quantify the number of CAs used at any particular time to minimize cost and maximize profit.

VRS is a relatively new and rapidly growing industry in the United States. Early experiments in VRS were conducted on a small scale in Texas in 1995 and in Arizona in the late 1990s and early 2000s; however, it was not until one corporation, Sorenson Communications, began distributing free videophones to the deaf community in 2003 that VRS became widespread. Access to videophone technology led increasing numbers of deaf people to use VRS for everyday telecommunication. As VRS grew, the deaf community began to learn ways to successfully manage their calls. Keating and Mirus (2003) note that effective communication via video technology requires that a person possess a number of skills, including "manipulation of desktop 'real estate,' manipulation of language features, manipulation of image transmission and body relations, creation of a radically different sign space, alteration of signing speed, increased repetition, code-switching, and adjustment of deictic references" (p. 700).

In sum, video streaming technology has dramatically influenced the manner in which deaf people access telecommunication and has shaped how interpreting services are provided to the deaf community. Further, VRS has impacted the relationship between deaf people and interpreters. Among these changes that have occurred since the advent of VRS was the establishment of a for-profit model for the provision of interpreting services.

THE PROFESSIONALIZATION OF INTERPRETING

Professionalization of a field occurs through a sequence of steps: (1) there is clear evidence of a need for the work to be performed on a full-time basis, (2) formal training is established for the work, (3) a professional association emerges to support the work, (4) formal political and/or legal support for the work (e.g., certification) is developed, and (5) a code of ethics emerges to guide the work (Wilensky, 1964). The act of interpreting has occurred since antiquity whenever people who use different languages come together, and for most of its history, interpretation has been viewed as a common and unexceptional activity (Pöchhacker, 2004). It has only been within the past 60 years that the practice of interpreting has manifested the characteristics of a profession.

The first step in professionalization is for society to recognize the need for particular types of work to be conducted on a full-time basis (Abbott, 1988; Wilensky, 1964). The need for full-time spoken language interpreters was recognized prior to the need for full-time signed language interpreters. For example, spoken language interpreters were employed for highly public international events such as the 1919 Paris Peace Conference (Cox, 2003); however, it was not until the Nuremberg Trials in 1945 and 1946 that interpreting gained widespread recognition (Gaiba, 1998). In this period, the Charter of the International Military Tribunal ruled that the defendants accused of war crimes during World War II had the right to a fair trial, including that proceedings be conducted in a language the defendant could understand. As a result of the tribunal's decree, the Nuremberg Trials were interpreted into four languages: German, English, Russian, and French (Cox, 2003; Gaiba, 1998). The Charter further mandated that the trial be carried out as expeditiously as possible in order to reduce expenses and time, as well as to maintain the attention of the public and the media (Cox, 2003; Gaiba, 1998). Thus, authorities decided that the trials would be interpreted simultaneously in real time. The use of simultaneous interpretation was a drastically different approach from how interpretations had been conducted in the past when they were either rendered consecutively or through the reading of pretranslated texts.

According to Gaiba (1998), simultaneous interpreting had not been a component of interpreter training prior to the Nuremberg Trials. Due to inexperience with this method, as well as a lack of familiarity with the system on behalf of all participants (e.g., judges and prosecutors), a series of mock trials or "dress rehearsals" were conducted prior to the actual Nuremberg Trials. Authorities overseeing the trials determined that an "interpreting monitor" would be needed at all times during the interpretation process to evaluate the accuracy of the interpretation. In addition, original testimony would be recorded for later review as needed. Gaiba noted that the use of simultaneous interpreting at the trials received widespread public recognition through media coverage and that simultaneous interpreting became widely used after the Nuremberg Trials.

In contrast to the historic events that spurred the development of spoken language interpreting, the origin of signed language interpreting had its roots as a social welfare activity for the benefit of deaf people (Napier, 2011). Prior to the professionalization of signed language interpreting, deaf people typically relied on volunteers including family members, friends, neighbors, teachers at residential schools for people who are deaf, and church workers to facilitate their communication with non-signers (Ball, 2013; Cokely, 1992, 2005). These volunteers offered their services as their schedules permitted and did not expect compensation (Fant, 1990). It is worth noting that members of the deaf community who were audiologically deaf and possessed strong bilingual skills also served as translators or interpreters by sharing information from newspapers, letters, or other sources with semilingual or monolingual deaf people (Stone, 2009). In reference to these early deaf interpreters, Adam, Carty, and Stone (2011) wrote, "The development of these skills is seen as part of their growth in cultural and linguistic awareness, of realising the possibilities of their language and the range of interconnections among and between Deaf people and the wider community" (p. 375).

The second step in the professionalization process, according to Wilensky (1964), is the development of training programs associated with the field. One of the first educational programs for spoken language interpreters, which focused on both consecutive interpretation and "whispered interpretation" (interpretation occurring within close proximity to people as opposed to through the use of equipment), was established in 1941 in Geneva, Switzerland (Gaiba, 1998). The establishment of early training programs, along with the Nuremberg Trials, resulted in increased awareness of spoken language interpretation as a professional activity. In the United States, recognition of signed language interpreting came nearly two decades later. In the 1960s and 1970s a series of events took place in the United States that fostered the professionalization of ASL–English interpreters. First, in 1964, the Registry of Interpreters for the Deaf (RID)[1] was established as the national organization for signed language interpreters. This represented a turning point for signed language interpreting because it created an entity to serve as an organizational hub for the work (step 3 in Wilensky's [1964] professionalization process). RID's aim was to recruit, educate, and maintain a list of qualified interpreters. In this way, the founders of RID established themselves as a select group of professionals who could identify the necessary skills of an interpreter and, thus, effectively produce quality interpreters. In 1972, RID expanded its goals to include establishment of certification standards (step 4 in Wilensky's [1964] professionalization process). Further, RID began to establish a small body of professional literature related to interpretation. The next step, developing a system of certification for interpreters, further supported the professionalization of interpreting by designating RID as gatekeepers to the field. By instituting a national certification process, RID was making a statement to society that it could assess individuals' qualifications for providing interpreting services.

At the same time, services to assess, identify, and support people with disabilities slowly emerged in the late 1960s and throughout the 1970s (step 4 in Wilensky's [1964] professionalization process). Prior to the establishment of laws such as the Individuals with Disabilities Education Act (IDEA), children with disabilities were often inaccurately assessed and inappropriately labeled (U.S. Department of Education, 2007). Accommodations that supported student learning were either nonexistent or ineffective. The Vocational Rehabilitation Act Amendments of 1965 ensured that deaf clients who received services from the Department

---

1. The Registry of Interpreters for the Deaf was originally named the National Registry of Professional Interpreters and Translators for the Deaf (Fant, 1990).

of Vocational Rehabilitation (DVR) were provided access to communication in the workplace, primarily through interpreting services. The 1973 Rehabilitation Act mandated reasonable accommodations for persons with disabilities in employment and required that organizations receiving federal funds (e.g., government agencies and state colleges) create conditions of equal access for all. In addition, the Education for All Handicapped Children Act of 1975, which called for the "free appropriate public education" of children in the "least restrictive environment," spurred the inclusion of deaf children in mainstream public classrooms with interpreting services. The passage of the Education for All Handicapped Children Act resulted in an immediate and enormous demand for signed language interpreters in K–12 educational settings.

Prior to the passage of legislation mandating access for deaf people, as well as subsequent case law (e.g., *Board of Education of Hendrick Hudson Central School District v. Amy Rowley*),[2] formal interpreter education was rare. The first courses in signed language and interpreter education in the United States were offered in 1948 as electives at the Central Bible College of Springfield, Missouri, with the goal of training students to become ministers, teachers of religion, or interpreters in religious settings (Ball, 2013). With the enactment of federal legislation in the 1970s, the demand for qualified interpreters skyrocketed, along with the scramble for interpreter training materials.

The growth of interpreter education can also be linked to the growing number of educational opportunities for deaf students, which increased the demand for interpreting services. Since 1864, Gallaudet University has provided a liberal arts education for deaf students seeking postsecondary education. Educational options began to expand in the 1960s and 1970s. In 1968, the National Technical Institute for the Deaf (NTID) was established within the Rochester Institute of Technology (RIT), resulting in an influx of deaf students who sought advanced technical training. At

---

2. The parents of kindergartener Amy Rowley requested that a qualified signed language interpreter be provided for all of Amy's academic classes. They were denied both by the school and in a subsequent independent hearing. Finally, the District Court for the Southern District of New York ruled that Amy was not receiving a "free and appropriate education" given that she was not learning all that she could learn in class if she did not have a handicap and that she was not performing up to her potential without an interpreter (*Board of Education of Hendrick Hudson Central School District v. Amy Rowley*, 1982).

its inception, three full-time interpreters were hired to facilitate communication (Ball, 2013). Given the scarcity of formal training and the high demand for interpreters at the time, RIT began to train hearing students to be interpreters for deaf students (Nowell & Stuckless, 1974). During the summer of 1969, six interpreting students, who were learning both ASL and interpreting skills, stayed on campus along with several deaf students who were also pursuing degrees. The successful development of the students' interpreting skills was attributed to their daily use of ASL with their deaf peers (Ball, 2013). In addition, this experience illustrated that advancements in educational opportunities for deaf people are intrinsically linked to the availability of interpreters.

In 1972, Gallaudet College (now Gallaudet University) also experienced an increase in need for qualified interpreters. The demand was driven by at least two factors: (a) the establishment of Gallaudet's continuing adult education program, resulting in the arrival of new deaf students and a need for additional interpreters, and (b) participation in the Washington Consortium of Colleges and Universities, which allowed Gallaudet students to take courses at nearby institutions through the use of interpreters (Riekehof, 1974). In response to this growing demand, Gallaudet began offering evening courses in beginning interpreting and reverse interpreting, which was outlined as "A study of the principles and problems of interpreting the manual, oral and written communications of deaf persons into their spoken or written equivalents" (cited in Ball, 2007, p. 62).

Similarly, California State University, Northridge (CSUN) began offering summer interpreting workshops in the early 1970s. Although these workshops supported the work of experienced interpreters, they were ineffective for novices (Fant, 1974). Fant attributed the lack of success to students' lack of mastery in ASL. In 1972, CSUN reevaluated and began to offer interpreter training as a series of four courses to be taken over 2 years. The first two semesters focused on developing ASL fluency, and the third semester emphasized translation, linguistics, and sign systems (such as Signing Exact English). The final semester provided a practicum experience for the students (Fant, 1974).

Due to the scarcity of qualified interpreters to fill the growing demand for services, the Vocational Rehabilitation Act of 1973 was amended to include grant funding for nonprofit organizations or agencies to establish interpreter training programs (U.S. Equal Employment Opportunity Commission, 1978). These programs were established at colleges and universities throughout the country, including Ohlone College, University of Arizona, and Seattle Central Community College. This financial support and the resulting development of interpreter training programs led to discussion of the requirements for entry and completion of these programs (Carter & Lauritsen, 1974; Nowell & Stuckless, 1974). Simultaneously, the first process model was developed for signed language interpreters, which was used in interpreter training programs (Ingram, 1974).

As stated earlier, another shift toward professionalization was the establishment of RID in 1964, resulting in other changes in the practices of interpreters working with the deaf community (e.g., certification, training, development of a code of ethics). RID's original mission was to recruit, educate, and maintain a list of qualified interpreters; however, that mission has greatly expanded since its inception (RID, 2015a). Presently, the mission of RID includes: (a) encouraging the growth of the profession, (b) establishing a national standard of interpreter quality, (c) advocating for best practices in interpreting, (d) advocating for professional development, and (e) educating the public about the role of interpreters and transliterators[3] (RID, 2015a). Establishing a national organization dedicated to these tasks situates the RID in a position of power and creates an "asymmetry of expertise" (Abbott, 1988, p. 5). For example, the public announcement that RID established a national standard of interpreter quality assumes that the organization is solely qualified to judge quality. Liljegren (2012) writes that professions are often depicted using terms associated with landscape (e.g., territory, turf, borders, boundaries, gatekeeping). In this way, the existence of a professional organization serves to establish boundaries (Liljegren, 2012) and discourage practitioners from performing work if they are not yet a part of the formal organization (Carr-Saunders & Wilson, 1933). Professional organizations persuade society to believe that "no one should be allowed to wear a professional title who has not been conferred it by an accredited

---

3. Kelly (2001) defined transliteration as the act of "delivering the signed message based on English grammatical order; basing sign choices on ASL usage, not English gloss; maintaining the meaning and intent of the original English; and understanding that the meaning of the message is more important than the form" (p. 2). Kelly noted that transliteration may be a Deaf person's preferred method for receiving messages in certain settings in order to access the language used by hearing conversational participants and be able to respond using similar language.

professional school" (Greenwood, 1957, p. 49). A national interpreting organization taking responsibility for establishing standards for practitioner quality is a form of gatekeeping admission to the profession and is a mechanism of control.

Another example of RID's influence on the interpreting field is illustrated by the events of the 2001 RID national conference, during which a motion was put forth that ASL interpreters must hold a bachelor's degree prior to taking the RID certification exam (Brunson, 2006). Brunson (2006) recalled that proponents of the motion argued that interpreting should be considered a profession and that a minimum educational requirement for an interpreter would, among other benefits, raise the status of interpreters. Brunson (2006) noted that the motion, passed in 2003 by the membership, initially was publicly denounced by some interpreters who had learned to interpret through direct connection to the deaf community (e.g., Codas)[4] rather than through a formal education. Similar to other fields that have advanced over the years (e.g., early childhood education, nursing), the pursuit of professionalization has significantly influenced the field of interpreting by imposing gatekeeping mechanisms such as education and national certification.

Another layer of control over interpreter education can be seen in the establishment of the Commission on Collegiate Interpreter Education (CCIE) in 2006 (CCIE, 2015), 5 years after the RID national conference motion proposed that interpreters must hold a bachelor's degree in order to take RID's national certification exam. The CCIE described their mission as follows:

> The mission of the CCIE is to promote the professionalism of the field of interpreter education through:
>
> • The accreditation of professional preparation programs,
> • The development and revision of interpreter education standards
> • The encouragement of excellence in program development,

---

4. Children of Deaf Adults (CODA) is an international organization whose members grew up with at least one deaf parent. The specific experiences of members vary (e.g., communication methods, family personalities), but members of CODA are united by their common identities (Preston, 1994). Not all hearing children of Deaf parents are members of the formal CODA organization; however, some may identify as Codas given their knowledge of Deaf culture and ASL (Padden & Humphries, 1988).

- A national and international dialogue on the preservation and advancement of standards in the field of interpreter and higher education, and
- The application of the knowledge, skills, and ethics of the profession. (2015)

Greenwood (1957) argues that regulating the training of professionals often takes the form of instituting accrediting processes that training programs must follow in order to achieve the status of being accredited. The CCIE accreditation process requires that interpreter education programs first submit a letter of intent, application, and Self-Study Report, along with payment of an application fee. This is followed by peer review of the Self-Study Report and a site visit conducted by a CCIE-trained rater (CCIE, 2015). Greenwood argues that accreditation practices are a mechanism used by professions to regulate schools in regard to number, location, curriculum content, and quality of instruction. Taken together, the increase in demand for interpreters, legislative action, educational opportunities, the development of a professional association, and the accreditation of interpreter education led to the professionalization of signed language interpreting in the United States over a 50-year period.

In one cautionary note that alludes to the historic dangers of a hierarchical approach to a profession, Brunson (2006) argues that the effort to encourage the growth of the interpreting profession may have had both positive and negative impacts on the deaf community as well as interpreters themselves. Brunson (2006) writes that, historically, "in the days of guilds, although members had a say in who and how one becomes a member, it was the king who was the ultimate ruler of the guild" (p. 7). Brunson argues that, as with the work of physicians, it is likely that government-initiated regulatory policies will be developed to govern the work of interpreters if the field is considered a profession. While the national organizations of interpreters (such as RID) will act as gatekeepers to the profession (e.g., membership, certification), government regulations (e.g., state and national requirements) will emerge to regulate interpreting services. In addition, Brunson (2006) writes that the deaf community should not be perceived as "passive receivers of information [but rather] an integral part of the interpreting process" (p. 8). Historically, the deaf community determined whether an individual demonstrated appropriate skill, knowledge, and trustworthiness to provide interpreting services (Cokely, 2005). Brunson (2006) suggests that advancing ASL–English interpreters to the status of professionals fails to position deaf consumers of interpreting services as experts in the services they receive.

Research that examines the dynamics of professions has resulted in several frameworks that can be applied to the development of signed language interpreting as a profession. If interpreting is to be regarded as a profession, and those who perform this service as professionals, then the assumption is that interpreters have an advanced degree, are certified, and are experts in the practice. Over time, interpreting work has been organized in a manner that distinguishes it from other occupations. In the following section, I argue that the growing status of signed language interpreters as professionals is not the same as that of CAs who work in VRS.

VIDEO RELAY SERVICE: A PROFESSION?

One may argue that signed language interpreting has satisfied the criteria of professionalization set forth by Wilensky (1964); however, that argument becomes clouded for interpreters who work in the VRS setting. I do not claim here that the work of VRS CAs does not meet any of the steps in the professionalization process. In fact, two of the steps in Wilensky's professionalization process have been achieved: clear evidence of the need for the work to be done full time and legal support for the job. The FCC serves as the legal backbone supporting VRS. In current FCC guidelines, 80% of VRS calls must be answered by a CA within 120 seconds; further, the FCC states that VRS must be offered as a 24-hour service (FCC, n.d.). These requirements evidence a need for CAs to work in VRS full time, satisfying the first step in Wilensky's professionalization process. In addition, the FCC's legal authority over reimbursement and approval of providers, among other things, satisfies step 4 in Wilensky's professionalization process.

The second step in Wilensky's (1964) professionalization process is the development of formal training in work practices. Greenwood (1957) adds that formal education in the United States is delivered via a large educational complex. The education of signed language interpreters unfolded in the context of college programs such as Gallaudet University, CSUN, and NTID (Fant, 1974; Riekehof, 1974). As stated earlier, the prerequisite of completing a bachelor's degree prior to taking the national interpreter certification exam was put in place by the RID membership in 2003 (Brunson, 2006). Conversely, in many VRS companies, CAs are not required to hold national certification or have formal training in the field. In fact, the largest VRS provider, for whom 90% of CAs in the United States work, currently does not require certification or formal education prior to hire; rather, applicants are screened and trained within the corporate system. CAs may have minimal or no professional experience as an interpreter prior to being hired; it is expected that they learn, with support, on the job.

The VRS system is similar to other businesses that have seen rapid growth. For example, prior to the Industrial Revolution, U.S. society had limited production and was a predominantly agricultural economy, with limited division of labor and minimal variation in social class (Morrison, 2006). Preindustrial life consisted of physically exhausting work, poverty, and short life spans (Volti, 2008). Advancements in manufacturing technology led to the migration of the population from rural to urban areas in search of employment in factories. As a result, two new socioeconomic classes emerged: factory workers and their employers (Volti, 2008). In addition, the introduction of large-scale industrial organization led to the need for other occupations such as accountants, secretaries, and insurance brokers (Carr-Saunders & Wilson, 1933). Managing workers became a scientific process aimed at increasing efficiency in order to bolster profit.

The introduction of large organizations of service provision has increased exponentially since this period (Brophy, 2011). Today, around the world, people demand faster service at cheaper prices, a phenomenon that has been labeled "The McDonaldization of Society" (Ritzer, 2008, p. 1). In Ritzer's (2008) view, corporations such as McDonald's have succeeded because they offer "consumers, workers, and managers efficiency, calculability, predictability, and control" (p. 13). Ritzer's points refer to the speed at which a want or need is fulfilled in a standardized, controlled, and measurable manner. In an effort to be efficient, McDonald's restaurant employees are given specified tasks that do not require decision making. In this system, employees are dehumanized and considered equivalent to robots, with work that is often constrained, monotonous, and highly scripted, leading to boredom with the routine and ultimately to a decrease in quality of work (Ritzer, 2008). Furthermore, a younger population of employees is recruited to work in this setting because they are willing "to surrender their autonomy to machines, rules, and procedures . . . relatively untrained employees are more easily controlled by the nonhuman technology" (Ritzer, 2008, pp. 118–119). The conditions described by Ritzer are not unlike those of VRS, in which untrained CAs yield their autonomy to VRS providers, as can be seen in the employment and in-house training of new ASL–English interpreters in VRS.

Although the Industrial Revolution changed the manager's perception of the worker in reference to physical labor, the same shift can be seen in the perception managers have of those who perform "mental labor," such as in accounting departments or specialized technical teams within a corporation (Brophy, 2011, p. 411). According to Brophy, characteristics of mental labor include routinizing, deskilling, and dehumanizing brain work. The work performed by CAs can be further described as "cognitive capitalism," in which the product is not tangible, but rather the result of information, knowledge, and communication (Brophy, 2011, p. 410). In such an environment, management controls the planning, organization, review, and record keeping associated with mental labor, whereas workers (and often lower ranked supervisors) blindly perform their work. Mental labor is specifically organized by managers into a set of repetitive tasks for employees. Call center work is an example of mental labor. Brophy (2011) described call center work as "the production of communication by means of communication" (p. 412). Call centers are established in centralized offices dedicated to the purpose of participating in a high quantity of phone calls for an organization (e.g., technology support, debt collection). Call centers emerged in America in the 1980s and subsequently spread throughout the 1990s as a means of "mediating the relationship between the institutions and the subjects of cognitive capitalism, gauging public opinion, offering us assistance through technological mishaps, and registering our numerous complaints" (Brophy, 2011, p. 412). Call centers follow a for-profit model in which the goal is to maximize profit while minimizing costs (Taylor & Bain, 1999). Describing the logistics of call center work, Taylor and Bain (1999) write:

> Predictive dialing systems work their way through databases of customers' phone numbers and, in accordance with programmed requirements, automatically dial the number, connecting operator to customer. Prior to, or at the precise moment of connection, the relevant customer details appear on the screen enabling the agent to make informed communication. In outbound operations the onus is placed upon the agent to either sell, or create interest in, a particular product or service. (p. 108)

CAs in VRS work in similar environments as call center employees. An automated system controls incoming calls, and at the precise moment of connection, the customer's information (e.g., phone number and self-determined username) appears on the screen. In addition, by applying Brophy's (2011) description of work in call centers (e.g., logistics, conditions of work), the work of VRS CAs can be seen to meet similar conditions. For example, CAs are stationed in a centralized office where their job is to process a large quantity of calls, CAs work in a for-profit environment where their work is evaluated quantitatively based on production, and the CAs' work is structured in a way that detaches them from the planning, organization, and review of the work. Instead, the CA is engaged in highly repetitive tasks, such as interpreting calls one after another in rapid succession.

According to Moser-Mercer (2003), interpreters who work at a distance from their consumers report feelings of reduced control over their work due to their physical detachment from the conversational participants. This is not surprising given the high psychological demands and the decreased decision latitude associated with working in call centers in general (Charbotel et al., 2008). Call centers provide an example of a workplace that combines service with capitalism, creating a mismatch between the needs of the employee and corporate expectations. Martí-Audí, Valverde, and Heraty (2013) recognize that call centers are not entirely one-size-fits-all and propose a "bird cage model" of human resource management for call centers. Martí-Audí et al. (2013) argue that the constant measurement of employee performance (e.g., answer time, call abandonment, or unanswered calls) and the clear constraints on professional autonomy present in call center work might vary from call center to call center; however, the overall control present in human resource management (the bars of the bird cage) are still present in all cases. Studies of call center management align with the management of CAs in VRS. The performance tracking of four call centers in Spain, as depicted by Martí-Audí et al. (2013), parallels the practice of performance tracking of CAs in VRS. The standardization of work in call centers and the constraints placed on professional autonomy associated with a for-profit business model of human resource management are evident in VRS.

The daily practices of CAs in VRS reflect a highly structured process. VRS work takes place at a single location, in which CAs are often identified by a number and encouraged to interpret all incoming calls for a period of time, whether they self-identify as qualified or not. CA success is often measured solely by statistical reports of efficiency that show the time required to answer a call, the number of minutes "on a call," the number of transferred calls, the amount of time working in a team, and the length of breaks. The conditions vary across video relay providers; however, analysis of these variables is a frequent evaluation of performance in VRS settings. As a result, CAs report becoming more concerned with their statistical reports than with the quality of the service they provide. For example, if a CA feels that continuing to interpret a call would be impossible, the VRS provider recommends that the CA either request a team or transfer the call; however, for some VRS providers, these actions are documented and will show up in a report of the CA's efficiency and have historically influenced CAs' ability to obtain future hours of work (Alley, 2014). The use of efficiency reports may subtly—or not so subtly—reinforce the distinction between management and those who perform mental labor.

As stated earlier, a professional is characterized as an expert. It is expected that the professional follow a moral compass with the best interest of the client in mind, as opposed to the pursuit of personal gain (Flynn, 2009; Parsons, 1939; Wilensky, 1964). At the macro level, VRS inarguably functions under a capitalist for-profit model of service provision, with minimal regard for the quality of the service provided. This can be seen in the call center environment in which CAs work, the numbers-based model used to assign interpreters, the rewards-based motivation of workers, and the quantitative nature in which they are assessed. Factors such as these influence the professional autonomy of CAs, creating an environment in which they do not have the decision latitude to use professional judgment to make decisions regarding their work.

Chapter 2

Professional Autonomy and Video Relay Service

Drawing on characteristics advanced by Kasher (2005) and Sandstrom (2007), professional autonomy can be defined in two ways: (a) The ability of a person to use reason and ethics to guide one's own actions, and (b) the freedom granted from the professional community, as well as from the society in which one works, to make decisions and act in a particular manner. I argue that video relay service (VRS) call centers are organized in a way that restricts the individual professional autonomy of communications assistants (CAs) through the highly structured management of work in an attempt to standardize service provision and increase profit.

Limited professional autonomy is not unique to the work of interpreters in VRS. Proponents of capitalist production, in general, view human decision making as a threat to the standardization of work and, ultimately, the opportunity for profit. In this approach, rationalization and bureaucracies supersede individual decision making (Sandstrom, 2007). Further, in an effort to minimize the threat of individual thought, the autonomy of employees working in various fields is restricted. These constraints are often framed by management as being "necessary and inevitable" for the success of the company (Braverman, 1998, p. 97).

American Sign Language (ASL)–English interpreting did not originally have a for-profit model of service provision. In fact, initially, interpreting was not considered a profession because interpreters were often the friends and family members of people within the deaf community and performed their work without pay, training, or formal positions. The interpreters held complete autonomy given the lack of organization and supervision of their work in the community. Kasher (2005) and Sandstrom (2007) describe *autonomy* as the ability of a person to use reason and ethics to guide one's own actions. Historically, in the absence of supervision, formal education, or a professional organization, interpreters made decisions in regard to their work guided by personal ethics and community standards. As stated earlier, a drastic demand for interpreters emerged after a series of legislative actions (e.g., Americans With

Disabilities Act of 1990; No Child Left Behind in 2001) propelled the advancement of communication access for deaf people in educational and employment settings. During this time, a series of philosophical models regarding the role of the interpreter emerged (e.g., machine/conduit, communication facilitator, bilingual-bicultural) (Witter-Merithew, 1986). It could be argued that the first model (machine/conduit) was a complete pendulum swing in the opposite direction from the full autonomy that interpreters previously held. In this model, interpreters were essentially invisible; they were not participants in an interaction and were expected to simply relay communication verbatim. Each subsequent model reflects the evolution of the way interpreters viewed the role of deaf and hearing conversational participants, linguistic and cultural norms of the time, and the interpreting profession's understanding of the power associated with their role. For example, the communication facilitator model framed the interpreter as the means of conveying a message between a sender and a receiver regardless of their method of communication, whether it be ASL or an invented sign system (Roy, 1993). Roy goes on to explain that, within the communication facilitator model, the interpreter must have the skill to assess the communication style of the deaf conversational participant, convey the content and style of a message, as well as the knowledge and preparation for each assignment. Toward the end of the 1970s, interpreters framed their work in terms of a bilingual-bicultural model, which emphasized the importance of acknowledging that language and communication cannot be separated from their cultural context (Roy, 1993). Whether or not these terms accurately characterize an interpreter's role, the greater point is that the models were developed through discussion among practitioners, recognizing the changing environment in which interpreting was occurring, rather than being externally imposed upon the profession.

As the profession of ASL–English interpreting continued to evolve, research about interpreting began to emerge. In an effort to contextualize signed language research within the larger field of interpreting, Metzger (2006) investigated the history of signed language interpreting studies and categorized her findings by decade, topic, and methodology. Metzger (2006) was able to draw parallels between research in spoken and signed language interpreting. Her findings show that early studies of signed language interpreting in the 1970s and 1980s focused on characteristics and skills associated with effective interpreters, as well as source-to-target language comparisons (Brasel, Montanelli, & Quigley, 1974; Schein,

1974). Soon thereafter, spoken language research highlighted interpreting in educational and conference settings (Seleskovitch, 1978). Subsequent studies included these topics but also examined more divergent topics as the field continued to grow.

Studies of community interpreting, including medical and legal settings, appeared in the 1980s and 1990s (Gustason, 1985; Mathers, 1999; Shaw, 1996). These studies focused on small-scale, interactive environments in structured settings. Additional research began to materialize that depicted interpreters as active participants in interpreted interactions, a perspective that drastically differed from the machine/conduit model of interpreters. For example, Roy (2000) examined ways in which interpreters moderated turn-taking, prompted turns between conversational participants, or handled overlapping talk. Using data collected from an interpreted meeting between a college professor and a graduate student, Roy shows that interpreters made decisions to participate in communication and that these decisions had direct impact on the outcome of an interaction in a postsecondary context.

In a later study, Metzger (1999) found that interpreters frequently took on the role of the author of communication, using devices known as *footing shifts*, rather than merely rendering information generated by the conversational participants. Interpreters created footing shifts by asking for clarification from one of the conversational participants, repeating phrases that were not repeated in the source, expanding on information, or indicating who was speaking or signing in a conversation. The tactics identified by Metzger (1999) demonstrate that interpreters were involved in rendering messages, again diverging from the machine/conduit model under which interpreters previously functioned. The machine/conduit model views the interpreter as a passive participant in communication tasked with conveying a message verbatim into the target language (Hsieh, 2014). Metzger (1999) shows that "interpreters are not merely impartial intermediaries facilitating dyadic interactions" (p. 23), as the conduit model had suggested; rather, they are participants in interpreted interactions and make decisions regarding their work.

These groundbreaking studies on interpreting discourse paved the way for new views of interpreting work: interpreters as autonomous decision makers. As participants in a communicative interaction, interpreters make decisions that require analysis of various aspects of the communicative event, including stressors that are present at the time of the interpretation and actions that can be used as a response. In considering potential actions that can be taken, interpreters assess the power (or lack of power) that they hold to alter their current situation. Professional power, granted by society based on its perception of an individual's role in the particular situation, is the foundation of professional autonomy (Sandstrom, 2007). Research that indicated that signed language interpreters have decision-making power was a precursor to the recognition of interpreters as autonomous professionals (Witter-Merithew, Johnson, & Nicodemus, 2010).

After Roy (2000) examined strategies used by interpreters to moderate turn-taking, Dean and Pollard (2001) created the demand-control schema adapted from Karasek's 1979 model. In their work, Dean and Pollard (2001) associated occupational stress with the activity of signed language interpreting by identifying demands and controls associated with interpreting work. In their reckoning, *demand* (linguistic, environmental, interpersonal, and intrapersonal) needs to be addressed for the success of an interpretation. The term *control* refers to the ability that an interpreter has to mitigate the demand. For example, an interpreter working in a medical setting may identify one demand as an inaccessible sight line between the deaf patient and the interpreter during a medical examination. A possible control may be to ask the doctor to explain the upcoming exam while the patient is still sitting and prior to the patient moving to the inaccessible position. The interpreter may continue determining further methods of communication as the patient's position changes.

Witter-Merithew, Johnson, and Nicodemus (2010) argued that the ability to make decisions regarding one's work and to address the demands identified within an interpreted event could only be achieved when the system supports the decision latitude of the interpreter. They offered the example of the interpreter in a courtroom setting being viewed as an expert who possesses thorough knowledge of legal proceedings and, as a result, is granted a great deal of decision latitude regarding the manner in which she provides interpreting service (e.g., requesting correction to the court record). In contrast, a CA in a VRS setting may have far less decision latitude due to the constraints placed on her work by both the FCC and the VRS providers (Witter-Merithew, Johnson, & Nicodemus, 2010). The FCC refers to interpreters as CAs, replacing the traditional label of interpreter, which may suggest that the professional autonomy traditionally exercised by interpreters may not carry over in the VRS setting. In addition, VRS providers limit the autonomy of CAs by imposing bureaucratic structures, such as productivity tracking, to daily work in VRS. The system-based constraints that govern the provision of interpreting in a VRS environment may limit the ability of

CAs to use professional autonomy and, thus, the controls they may use to address demands in other community-based interpreting environments.

Another factor in the establishment of VRS is the overwhelming quantity of CAs needed in order to provide VRS and the subsequent impact this has on its various stakeholders. One may argue that VRS has impacted interpreters as well as the deaf community in ways previously unheard of in history. Interpreters are flocking to VRS in pursuit of work that offers a variety of consumers, a regular salary, and limited travel requirements. This flight to VRS has resulted in a shortage of signed language interpreters who perform work in the community. Bailey (2005) stated,

> As long as I can remember there has been a shortage of interpreters—especially qualified, certified interpreters. In other fields, shortages normally equate to high demand followed by higher prices. In our field the shortage has mostly meant a lowering of qualification requirements to satisfy needs—or the dreaded warm body approach. (p. 15)

Staffing of VRS call centers has changed since its onset. Peterson (2011) observes that CAs were initially required to have a minimum of national certification and 5 years of experience before being hired; however, after a review of job announcements between the years 2005 and 2010, Peterson confirms that these requirements have changed. Peterson states that "'demand' is cited as the reason for making incredibly complex work the equivalent of entry-level employment" (2011, p. 209). Currently, many corporations screen CAs for minimal qualifications and then train them on the job. Furthermore, CAs are expected to improve their skills and become qualified on the job as they perform VRS work, rather than demonstrate a high level of skill prior to hiring. Lack of experience prior to being hired creates an environment in which CAs are less likely to exercise professional autonomy.

Often, CAs learn how to navigate the VRS system through a trial-and-error approach. Bocian (2012) applied Dean and Pollard's (2001) model of demands and controls to the work associated with VRS. His results suggest that the demands associated with VRS are different from situations in which all participants in an interpreted event are in the same location. In a series of focus group discussions, participants in Bocian's study expressed demands caused by the environment (e.g., computer screen pixelation and freezing), interpersonal protocol (e.g., company scripts), paralinguistic stressors (e.g., stakeholders' understanding of the subject), and intrapersonal responses to policies that govern the work (e.g., productivity reports). Participants in the study offer the controls that they have learned to exert in this setting in order to avoid burnout (e.g., work fewer hours, call a team, memorize the phone keypad). Taken together, studies that indicate interpreter participation in discourse settings (Metzger, 1999; Roy, 2000) and studies of decisions made using the demand-control schema (Bocian, 2012; Dean & Pollard, 2001) suggest that interpreters perceive themselves as having decision-making latitude in their work. Interpreters control turn-taking and use footing shifts to author interpreter-generated communication. This latitude is not evident in the governing structure of the work of CAs in a VRS environment.

Today, advancing frameworks argue for the autonomous decision making of signed language interpreters. Llewellyn-Jones and Lee (2013) state that the work of interpreters should be perceived through a three-dimensional model that is not governed by rules, but rather by "role-space" (p. 56) composed of three axes (Participant/Conversational Alignment, Interaction Management, and Presentation of Self). In their model, Llewellyn-Jones and Lee (2013) state that social interactions are fluid and interpreters need to respond to interactions as "human beings with well-honed social skills, sensitivities, and awareness" (p. 70).

Although the perception of the role of the interpreter is moving away from the machine model, current policies associated with work in VRS do not reflect this evolution. For example, in the community, an interpreter may decide not to accept a job interpreting for a family member due to personal conflict; however, for the largest VRS provider, the CA does not have the ability to reject a VRS call due to personal conflict. Instead, interpreters anecdotally report being advised to answer the call and let the deaf person decide whether he or she would like a different interpreter.

CAs employed in the VRS industry work within a system that constrains their work. They are charged with adhering to various—and sometimes conflicting—constraints mandated by the FCC or established by corporate VRS providers. These constraints are established to accomplish goals (e.g., earning profit, providing access, offering quality interpreting service), but the rules may conflict with one another. For example, offering quality interpreting service may mean spending extra time with a caller prior to initiating the call in order to learn more about the upcoming conversation. Such actions are supported by the Registry of Interpreters for the Deaf (RID) in the VRS Standard Practice Paper (2007b), which states that "interpreters are most successful when they are able to obtain information about the subject of an interpreted conversation in advance because interpreters exercise professional judgment and make decisions based, in part, on this information" (p. 2). Time spent working with a caller prior to connecting a call ensures the success of communication during the call and can be considered customer service—giving the caller time and undivided attention. However, given the profit-driven, potentially inadequate, staffing of centers by VRS providers, spending time obtaining information from a caller may be overshadowed by the goal of connecting calls quickly. Preparation time is not reimbursable by the FCC because the interpreter is not connected to both a deaf and hearing party. In addition, the time invested for the purpose of customer service delays connection with the next caller, who may have to wait for an available CA.

Comments elicited during a series of VRS interpreter focus groups held by the National Consortium of Interpreter Education Centers (2010) suggest that interpreters want to learn how to work effectively within a corporate structure in order to maintain quality of service while meeting the demands for increased quantities of service required by the VRS providers for the purpose of earning a profit. CAs frequently report strong feelings about the constraints placed on their professional autonomy and the impact of these constraints on the quality of their work. An example of this can be seen in the frequent discussion of the potential for burnout among CAs (Bower, 2013). In addition to the physical and mental labor associated with interpreting in a VRS environment, CAs can also be seen as performing emotional labor. Hochschild (1983) uses the term *emotional labor* in reference to "the management of feeling to create a publicly observable facial and bodily display" (p. 6). Taylor and Bain (1999) apply Hochschild's idea of emotional labor to the work of call center employees, who are given instructions such as that their smile should be auditorily evident to the caller. They argue that there is continuous pressure placed on the employee to "successfully" complete each call to the satisfaction of the customer and quickly begin the next call. Success of the call center representative is measured quantitatively. Taylor and Bain (1999) offer the following example:

> In one insurance company, where agents were expected to convert one in six calls into policies, a particularly acute source of stress emanated from the fact that all calls received were counted against the operator, even general enquiries which could not be translated into sales. (pp. 109–110)

Continuous managerial surveillance and the monotony and repetitiveness of the work are sources of stress for call center employees. In contrast to other call center employees, CAs are tasked with providing customer service that is evident auditorily as well as visually. In a review of the 2008 Annual Complaint Summary (a compilation of VRS complaint logs published on the FCC website), Peterson (2011) notes that the most common complaints regarding VRS provision are related to poor CA etiquette and CA quality, which may lead CAs to believe that they can avoid complaints by smiling more. The action of assisting with communication, along with the expected smile and friendly persona required of VRS interpreters, despite the stress of the work, attitude of the callers, and fatigue, can be considered a type of emotional labor and regarded as an additional stressor for the CA. Furthermore, in relabeling interpreters as CAs and expecting them to perform based on customer approval ratings and efficiency reporting, it may be that they perceive their role as less autonomous and more formulaic or rule governed.

Sandstrom (2007) notes that "autonomy is a privilege and allows the professional to have greater influence over the everyday terms of his or her work" (p. 99). When professionals work within a large system, their autonomy is often limited. Major (2013) refers to relational work and rapport management in her study of interpreters in the healthcare setting. Relational work refers to the work that all people do to maintain relationships during an interaction. Major offers examples of relational work in healthcare interactions such as the use of indirect questions when speaking to the doctor (e.g., "Could you?"), apologizing when asking for clarification, and softening devices (e.g., "just"). Major argues that "experienced interpreters engage in and actively facilitate relational work to such a degree that it should be considered an integral part of the healthcare interpreter's role" (p. xiii). This type of relational work may be compared with the emotional labor that occurs in call centers. Arguably, VRS CAs work under similar institutional conditions as call center representatives, and organizational constraints may limit the professional autonomy of CAs.

HISTORY OF TELECOMMUNICATIONS IN THE UNITED STATES

The invention of the telephone dramatically changed the way people functioned (see Appendix A for timeline of telecommunications). In the early 1870s, while working at the Boston School for Deaf Mutes,

Alexander Graham Bell attempted to create a device that would produce a visual response to sound. Historical records indicate that Bell, "hoped that the deaf could speak into such devices and gain visual feedback of the sounds they were producing—and that this would help them to develop speech" (Mercer, 2006, p. 31). In his work toward this goal, Bell unexpectedly developed the basic technology of the telephone. Telephone technology greatly altered the speed and efficiency at which people could communicate, but despite Bell's original intent, for most deaf people, the telephone was nothing more than "a useless piece of plastic and metal" (Lang, 2000, p. 5).

Robert Weitbrecht, James Marsters, and Andrew Saks adapted the TTY in the late 1960s to make the telephone system accessible to the deaf community (Lang, 2000). "There is no better term than 'behemoths' to describe the first teletypewriters (TTYs) Deaf people used to make phone calls. The enormous, old, and heavy machines . . . weighed several hundred pounds" (Lang, 2000, p. 3) (see Figure 1).

Over time, TTY technology improved, and the device eventually became a much smaller, portable unit (see Figure 2). Nearly 100 years

The Teletype Corporation Model 28 ASR teletypewriter was a first generation TTY. It weighed 260 pounds and measured 39" × 36" × 18". From the collection of I. Lee Brody, courtesy of NY-NJ Phone-TTY, Inc.; photograph by George Potanovic, Jr./Sun Studios.

FIGURE 1. *Historical photo and description of early teletypewriter. Used with permission of Rochester Institute of Technology. All rights reserved.*

FIGURE 2. *A portable TTY.*

after its invention, the telephone was finally modified into a technological device that was functional for deaf people.

With this new communication technology emerged new opportunities for deaf people. Lang (2000) asserts that the TTY provided deaf people an increased sense of independence and also cultivated a sense of "empowerment, cohesiveness, and cultural enlightenment" (p. ix) within the deaf community. However, in the 1960s, TTYs were still considered "a novelty, and out of reach in price and accessibility to the working-class Deaf people" (Padden & Humphries, 2005, p. 87). Few owned the device, and therefore, deaf people's access to telecommunication remained limited. Agencies in California began offering text relay service using volunteer operators who read the teletype message from the deaf caller to the hearing caller and typed the response to the deaf caller (Padden & Humphries, 2005). Due to varying levels of English proficiency within the deaf community, some deaf people considered the TTY and text relay service to be inconvenient and ineffective (Brunson, 2011). To alleviate this challenge, some interpreting agencies offered specified periods of time where deaf people could come into the agency and interpreters would be available to interpret phone calls; however, this was not common practice. Regardless

FIGURE 3. *Faculty member Warren Goldman using a Vistaphone on NTID Campus. Used with permission of Rochester Institute of Technology. All rights reserved.*

of its limitations, the TTY was seen by many as an important step toward the development of policies in support of products and services for individuals with disabilities in the United States (Lang, 2000).

In the 1960s, Bell Laboratories announced the development of the Picturephone, a device that offered visual access between conversational participants. In 1973, the National Technical Institute for the Deaf (NTID) in Rochester, New York installed 20 picturephones on its campus (see Figure 3).

The original Picturephone consisted of four parts:

> A 12-button Touch-Tone telephone; a display unit, with picture tube, camera tube, and a loudspeaker built in; a control unit, which contains a microphone; and a service unit containing power supply, logic circuits, and transmission equalizing circuits, which is installed out of sight. (Dorros, 1969, p. 138)

Bell Laboratories advertised the Picturephone as a valuable addition to business communication, specifically marketing it to large corporations as a means through which workers could share graphs, documents, and objects visually from a distance. The major concern regarding the Picturephone was its inability to discriminate between essential portions of a visual picture and the auxiliary space in which no information is being shared (such as the corners of the screen). Twenty years after its initial development, British Telecom and the University of Essex announced the creation of video technology clear enough to support the understanding of signed language through video communication ("Telephones Come to Terms," 1989). This technology transmitted only the moving parts of a video picture as opposed to continuously transmitting static portions. Reducing the amount of information being transmitted resulted in a clearer picture.

According to the Individuals with Disabilities Enabling Advocacy Link (IDEAL) group (a not-for-profit organization associated with AT&T that focuses on the employment of individuals with disabilities), the history of VRS can be traced to 1991 when Steve Jacobs was appointed Chairman of the AT&T initiative known as Project Freedom (IDEAL Group, 2012). VRS was developed as a method for deaf and hearing individuals to communicate with one another at a distance via an interpreter (see Figure 4 for a current schema of VRS technology).

The aim of the IDEAL Group's Project Freedom was to implement interactive video technology for use with signed language communication over the telephone. Testing of the video technology began in 1994 when a class of students from Horace Mann Montessori School for the Deaf in Dayton, Ohio, used AT&T Project Freedom's Vistium Video Systems

FIGURE 4. *Schema of video relay service technology. Source: FCC.*

to communicate with their teachers. In 1995, Sprint initiated the first trial runs of VRS in Austin, Texas, through four public call centers. Later, in 1997, a second trial began serving 10 cities in Texas. The same year, James Lee Sorenson, of Sorenson Media, unveiled a new compression and decompression tool called "Codec," which was designed to reduce bandwidth requirements while maintaining video quality (Sorenson Media, n.d.). Apple, Adobe, and other corporate leaders quickly adopted this new technology. VRS became available throughout Texas in 2000; however, during this time, Sorenson Media partnered with D-Link to create the DVC-1000 and later the VP-100 videophones. In April 2003, Sorenson began distributing videophone technology to deaf people across the United States at no cost.

Overall, the development and distribution of videophones led to the rapid expansion of the video interpreting industry in the United States. The explosion of VRS changed the way that deaf people communicate and, subsequently, the provision of interpreting services.

INTERPRETERS AND TELECOMMUNICATION

Streamed video technology has greatly altered the way that interpreting services are provided to deaf consumers. Because of video technology, interpreting is no longer conducted solely under face-to-face conditions, but may also be delivered in a two-dimensional video format with interlocutors at a distance. Although it may be argued that the advance of telecommunications technology through the years has transformed the lives of both deaf and hearing people, the introduction of technological advancements is not without risk. Postman (1992) suggests that a primary danger in technology is that it presents itself as a friend, making the user's life easier. In this vein, "technology is seductive when what it offers meets our human vulnerabilities" (Turkle, 2011, p. 1). However, over time, technology changes our perception of human interactions. It also alters society's view of labor in terms of the value placed on efficiency, standardization, objectivity, measurement, expertise, and progress (Postman, 1992). In Postman's perspective, technology leads to management's belief that workers should not use their subjectivity when making decisions. To ensure efficiency and earn profit, standardization is considered best practice by corporations. As Postman states, "machines eliminate complexity, doubt, and ambiguity. They work swiftly, they are standardized, and they provide us with numbers that you can see and calculate with" (1992, p. 93). In a highly mechanized capitalist world, success is measured in terms of statistical benchmarks, which are assumed to be entirely objective.

Technology has also affected how we conduct our social lives (e.g., Skype, FaceTime, Facebook), although the use of social technology may also foster a sense of detachment from others. Turkle (2011) states, "Technology makes it easy to communicate when we wish and to disengage at will" (p. 13). This perspective is reflected in the way that remote interpreting is delivered. Moser-Mercer (2003) investigated the impact of remote interpreting by filming interpreters working in both remote and on-site environments at a conference. One interpretation was conducted while the interpreter was present at the event, while the other occurred via a remote location for the same event. Each of the interpreters in this study was filmed working in both environments. Results showed that the quality of the remote interpretation declined significantly after 30 minutes of interpreting, more so than interpretations rendered in the conference room. As a result of a series of interviews with the interpreters, Moser-Mercer asserts that one reason for the increase in the number of errors in a remote setting was due to a lack of presence at the interpreted event. She states, "The lack of proximity to clients and staff produces a feeling of alienation that ultimately results in lack of motivation and hence produces a decrease in interpreting quality" (Moser-Mercer, 2003, p. 9). Being situated at a distance from the communication event may create a feeling of having little control over the work, as well as an inability to identify with the audience who is relying on the interpretation.

Research suggests a number of other constraints for interpreters working in a remote setting. For example, physical constraints are placed on interpreters working from a separate location, such as with spoken language interpreters who interpret conference proceedings from a soundproof booth. In a study of spoken language interpreters, Roziner and Shlesinger (2010) state that interpreters expressed a need for feedback from the audience in order to determine if they were interpreting effectively. The authors note that without a visible audience, remote interpreters reported that they felt as though no one was paying attention to their interpretation, which led to a decrease in motivation. When interpreting for VRS, CAs are limited to visual access with only one conversational participant. The hearing individual on the call cannot be seen, and therefore, the CA only receives audible feedback. In addition, CAs do not have control over the visual input that they receive from the deaf caller. They are limited to the camera's range of view and deaf callers' positioning of the camera in relation to themselves. The CA also cannot control the quality of the image that is being transmitted, which may lead to frustration and a decrease in motivation.

The use of technology may impact the work of interpreters in a variety of ways. Prior to VRS, interpreters were individuals known in the deaf community they served (Fant, 1990); however, practically overnight, video interpreting changed interpreters' connection away from the local community. As a CA, the interpreter had become an anonymous individual initially identifiable only by a number. Dehumanizing the work further, managers quantitatively assess CA work based on the number of minutes they are logged in to their computer software and connected with a hearing and a deaf caller (Peterson, 2011). A frequently stated goal of VRS providers is for interpreters to achieve favorable efficiency statistics (i.e., those that produce the greatest profit). To measure the success of interpreters' work, VRS providers may collect data and generate statistical reports. Peterson (2011), a VRS interpreter, describes his experience with his VRS statistics: "The company keeps thorough statistics on every aspect of my work save one. The one thing the company does not concern themselves with is the quality of service I provide" (p. 214). His comment suggests that the profit-based motivation of VRS providers, coupled with the willingness of interpreters to work under these conditions, has dehumanized interpreters' work. CAs shift their attention from delivering quality interpretations to achieving the expected statistics of their VRS provider.

In the view of corporate VRS providers and the private investors that require a return on their investment, interpreter efficacy is often weighed in financial terms. The number of billable minutes a CA produces is a representation of efficiency and, thus, success. Just as the efficiency of a machine is assessed, management evaluates the work of CAs quantitatively. In this way, CAs may feel that they are merely another cog in the technology wheel, one that can be replaced with a faster and more profitable "part."

CONSTRAINTS ON THE WORK OF COMMUNICATIONS ASSISTANTS IN VRS

The work of CAs within the VRS setting is influenced by a number of external entities and systems. Governing documents either originate from federal mandates or agencies (e.g., Americans With Disabilities Act, FCC) or individual VRS corporations (e.g., Purple [acquired by ZVRS in 2017], Sorenson Communications, ZVRS). External controls are not unique to the VRS industry. Organizing forces are present in many types of systems in which interpreters work, including education, judicial, and healthcare systems. Meadows (2008) defines a system as "an interconnected set of elements that is coherently organized in a way that achieves something" (p. 11). Subsystems exist within larger institutional systems that serve their own function. For example, an accounting department is a microsystem that operates within a larger macrosystem—the organization under which it is housed. Similarly, individual VRS corporations function as a microsystem, governed by the macrosystem of governmental authority. Although the FCC establishes rules with the goal of communication access for deaf people, individual VRS providers establish rules with numerous goals, including monetary gain. This economic systemic structure is summarized by Smith's (2006) statement, "In contemporary global capitalist society, the 'everyday world' (the material context of each embodied subject) is organized in powerful ways by translocal social relations that pass through local settings . . . [which] carry and accomplish organization and control" (p. 17). Smith (2006) refers to organizational controls as "relations of ruling" (p. 17) that are frequently reflected in text-based documents, such as the rules outlined in FCC documents or the rules established by VRS providers that regulate the actions of CAs. In addition, materials delivered in ASL via video, such as training videos developed by VRS providers, can be considered as governing documents and organizational controls.

Technology, used as a medium to facilitate interpreted interactions, along with regulations carried over from prior telecommunications relay service (TRS) governance, act as catalysts for the change in interaction between interpreters and members of the deaf community. The dynamics of interactions are associated with the constraints placed on VRS interpreters by various governing bodies. To understand the impact of the videophone and VRS on the deaf community, the FCC needs to first be examined as a macrosystem:

> The FCC was established under the Communications Act of 1934, in an effort to regulate interstate and foreign commerce in communication by wire and radio so as to make available, so far as possible, to all the people of the United States, without discrimination on the

basis of race, color, religion, national origin, or sex, a rapid, efficient, nation-wide, and world-wide wire and radio communication service with adequate facilities at reasonable charges. (Communications Act, 1934, as amended by the Telecommunications Act, 1996)

Subsequently, Title IV of the Americans With Disabilities Act (ADA) of 1990, Section 225, was added to the Communications Act (1934), followed by the 21st Century Communications and Video Accessibility Act of 2010 signed by President Barack Obama on October 8, 2010. In the most recent legislation, TRS is defined as follows:

Telephone transmission services that provide the ability for an individual who is deaf, hard of hearing, deaf-blind, or who has a speech disability to engage in communication by wire or radio with one or more individuals, in a manner that is functionally equivalent to the ability of a hearing individual who does not have a speech disability to communicate using voice communication services by wire or radio. (21st Century Communications and Video Accessibility Act, 2010)

Functional equivalency is arguably the overarching goal of VRS according to both the ADA (1990) and the 21st Century Communications and Video Accessibility Act (2010). Perhaps to allow for flexibility in application, the law does not explicate the meaning of the phrase "functional equivalency" and, furthermore, does not provide a working definition of what it entails. In empowering the FCC to oversee that the goal of the ADA is carried out, Section 225 of the ADA lists a number of regulations pertaining to VRS. Of these regulations, the following pertain specifically to the work of interpreters:

The Commission shall, not later than one year after July 26, 1990, prescribe regulations to implement this section, including regulations that . . .

(E) prohibit relay operators from failing to fulfill the obligations of common carriers by refusing calls or limiting the length of calls that use telecommunications relay services;

(F) prohibit relay operators from disclosing the content of any relayed conversation and from keeping records of the content of any such conversation beyond the duration of the call; and

(G) prohibit relay operators from intentionally altering a relayed conversation. (ADA, 1990, Section 225)

These regulations may be summarized as confidentiality, accuracy, non-discrimination, and faithfulness of the interpretation. This document further asserts that the FCC can independently develop minimum standards as well as establish functional requirements, guidelines, and operational procedures for TRS. The FCC interpreted this legislation (outside of the clear rules stated) based on its understanding of functional equivalence.

The following are FCC rules about how CAs should proceed with VRS calls. These rules are found in the TRS Mandatory Minimum Standards (Telecommunication Relay Service Rules, 2011):

- The CA must continue with a call for a minimum of ten minutes.
- CAs are prohibited from intentionally altering the content of a relayed conversation.
- The CA must not refuse calls or limit the length of calls.
- The CA may not utilize a privacy screen and must disconnect from a call if the caller uses the privacy screen or is not responsive for greater than five minutes.
- The CA ID number must be announced to the Public Safety Answering Point (PSAP) or local emergency authority during a 911 call in order to ensure the ability to contact the CA if the call is disconnected.
- The TRS provider must make their best effort to accommodate the caller's preferred CA gender.

Peterson (2011) states that "VRS work does not qualify as interpreting as defined by interpreters collectively since 1964" (p. 200) and would be better described as "quick and educated guesses" (p. 203) made by CAs given the lack of prior knowledge that the CA possesses regarding who is talking to whom or why they are speaking. In fact, by referring to interpreters as CAs throughout FCC documents, the term *interpreter* is removed entirely. Labeling them "communications assistants" may foster the belief that interpreters are not language specialists, are easily interchangeable, and can be discarded or replaced by consumers at any time. In fact, this is logistically possible: CAs are present via a video format and can be accessed or disconnected at the click of a button.

This is not to say that interpreters have no influence over the direction that their role has taken in VRS; in fact, interpreters have been actively engaged in creating the working conditions of CAs. By agreeing to work for VRS providers that base success on interpreters' ability to produce profit, they accept their role as a CA. At the federal level, interpreters have an opportunity to be involved in the direction taken by the VRS industry. For example, the FCC website outlines ways that the community can be involved in FCC decision making:

> Gathering and analyzing comments from the public is an important part of the Federal Communications Commission's rulemaking process. The FCC considers the public's input when developing rules and policies. By submitting comments, the public can take part in developing policies that affect telecommunications and broadcast issues. (FCC, n.d.)

The website further explains how the FCC involves the public in the process of decision making. If an action is FCC initiated, the FCC will issue a public notice to inform the public and invite the public to comment within a given amount of time. In addition, an individual may submit a petition for rulemaking at any time. The petition is then available for public comment for a 30-day period. Other mechanisms to seek public input are available as well (e.g., notices of inquiry and proposed rulemaking).

In current practice, CAs must also be ready for any call at any time, quickly moving between medical, legal, social, education, business, and a variety of other topics. The unstated expectation of VRS providers is that CAs can interpret every call, a notion that is in opposition to the RID Code of Professional Conduct (CPC), which states interpreters are to "accept assignments using discretion with regard to skill, communication mode, setting, and consumer needs" (2005, p. 3). Given that, the CPC seems to not apply to the work of CAs in the VRS environment. CAs are expected to accept all calls within a limited amount of time and continue with them for a minimum of 10 minutes regardless of their perceived ability to interpret the call. In order for CAs to assess whether they are qualified to interpret a call, they would need time to discuss call content with the caller prior to connection—an action often prohibited by corporate rules. In addition, exercising professional discretion to select an assignment entails identifying instances in which a CA is not qualified to continue with a call, which may be prior to the 10-minute-on-call time constraint.

The constraints associated with working in a VRS setting often contrast with the fundamental precept of using professional discretion when accepting interpreting assignments. Brunson (2011) argues that an assumption has developed that the complex task of interpreting can be reduced into a one-size-fits-all formulaic action. This is supported by the use of preestablished scripts to guide a call, the structured technology to accept and/or complete a call, and the various ways that the CA is expected to log instances in which they deviate from their expected actions. By behaving as if there is a single way to progress through a VRS call, the humanity of the interpreter and the relationship that exists between interpreters and the deaf community go unrecognized.

Witter-Merithew et al. (2010) propose a model regarding how to function within systems: relational autonomy, which both recognizes the constraints imposed by legislative mandates and the systems that provide payment for interpreting services and recognizes the relationship of interpreters with the consumers of their services. Drawing on feminist theory, they assert that autonomy is socially constructed and "is achieved when the social conditions that support it are in place and give the practitioner—and consumers—the confidence to take charge of choices" (Witter-Merithew et al., 2010, p. 56). Presently, the VRS system significantly influences the decision latitude among CAs. CAs working in VRS must make conscious decisions to demonstrate practices that either adhere to the institutional systems or deviate from them when deemed necessary.

For example, the FCC requires VRS providers to "answer 80% of all VRS calls within 120 seconds. VRS providers must also offer the service 24 hours a day, seven days a week" (Telecommunications Relay Service Rules, 2011). Providers may attempt to successfully meet this FCC requirement while staffing the minimal number of CAs possible in order to earn a greater profit. One might assume that teaming with another CA to manage a challenging call is highly feasible given the number of interpreters in a single location. In fact, interpreters may choose to work for a VRS company in order to achieve a level of camaraderie and support that they do not receive when they work solely as a freelance interpreter. Anecdotal reports from CAs, however, suggest that team interpreting is discouraged by VRS companies in order to ensure that each CA is constantly producing billable minutes (Alley, 2014). A CA in this pilot study stated, "Right now there's a big crackdown against teaming. It costs twice as much to have a team there than it does to have one interpreter there" (Alley, 2014, p. 23). Another CA in the study summed up her experience with VRS interpreting as "a solo sport" (Alley, 2014, p. 23). It is true that when two CAs work together on a single call, the VRS company can only earn money from one call as opposed to if both CAs were working on separate calls and producing billable minutes. VRS providers may not develop guidelines that explicitly constrain the practice of teaming; however, the tracking of interpreters' requests for a team support a for-profit model of interpreting. Interpreters seem to be aware that if they request a team too frequently, there may be disciplinary actions such as the inability to reserve the shift that they prefer for an upcoming schedule. Teaming is one example of an overarching system that prioritizes profit and limits the autonomy of VRS interpreters.

The legal precepts that originate from the FCC, along with the profit-focused system in which VRS occurs, were the impetus for the study of professional autonomy and the decision-making of CAs. Toward this end, 20 CAs were interviewed using open-ended questions in order to illuminate their experiences in VRS (see Appendix B for details regarding methodology). Two major recurring themes emerged from data: tracking of CA work and customer service. The first theme suggests that CAs are influenced by their productivity being tracked by VRS providers (see Chapter 3). The second theme indicates that CAs' decisions are motivated by the goal of providing quality customer service (see Chapter 4). Following elements of a grounded theory methodology, I conclude that the two themes guide the decisions and professional autonomy of the CAs. These decisions are seen to occur within a VRS call as well as outside of a call. For example, decisions made outside of a VRS call (e.g., to accept a shift, to take a break) occur at the systemic level of the VRS practices. In contrast, decisions that take place during a VRS call (e.g., to ask for clarification, to call for a team) occur within the interpreted interactions of CAs and consumers of VRS services.

Although the interviews with the participants were extensive and varied, not all topics could be exhaustively discussed. For example, one participant who had worked as a CA for several years provided extensive discussion on the topic of burnout, whereas an interpreter new to VRS did not raise this as an issue. Thus, although themes that emerged during the interviews are provided in Table 1, the count reflects only those instances in which the topic was mentioned.

Emergent themes are factors that influence participants to respond by performing a variety of actions. For example, the desire to provide customer service sometimes leads CAs to skip scheduled breaks. The action of skipping a scheduled break is considered an action taken in response to the initial theme. Figure 5 illustrates the relationship between themes and actions.

The themes identified within the data are not mutually exclusive: CAs may reflect both themes in their decision-making process. Throughout this study, CAs often stated that they know their provider's expectations

Theme	Number of participants (N = 20)	Percentage of participants
Tracking of CA work	16	80%
Customer service	20	100%

regarding their productivity, but their decisions are largely influenced by their desire to provide customer service. CAs weigh the consequences of responding in a particular manner during the decision-making process. For example, CAs who recognize their need to call for a team during a complex medical call between a patient and nurse (i.e., customer service) will also consider how many times they had already called for a team that day (i.e., tracking of CA productivity) before arriving at a decision.

The following chapters intend to shed light on the decision-making of CAs, specifically highlighting the ways in which the tracking of CA work by VRS providers as well as the goal of providing customer service influences the decisions CAs make in this environment. Quotes from the interviews are used to illustrate their personal narratives and guide our understanding of the professional autonomy of interpreters in VRS.

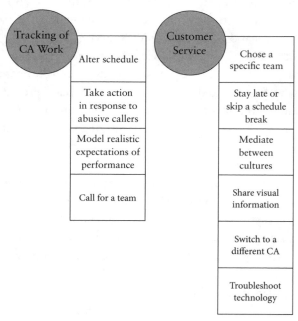

FIGURE 5. *Communications assistant actions in response to themes.*

Chapter 3

Provider Tracking of Communications

Assistant Work

A pilot study conducted by Alley (2014) suggests that communications assistants (CAs) were aware that rules existed governing their work; however, CAs may be unaware of the origin of the rules. Findings indicate that CAs followed the rules regardless of uncertainty of the origin of those rules. In this study, the CAs did not explain their reasons for abiding by the rules. This study explored this topic further by investigating instances in which CAs decided either to adhere to or deviate from video relay service (VRS) work rules. Furthermore, the study uncovered actions used by CAs in response to the rules governing CA work.

Throughout the interviews, participants often referred to *numbers*, *stats*, *percentages*, and *billable minutes*. CAs used these terms in reference to the efficiency reports used by some VRS providers to track CA work. According to participants, efficiency reports are a compilation of percentages that show the proximity (or distance) from the VRS provider's expectations of their productivity. The report may track such figures as (a) the speed at which a CA answers, (b) how rapidly the CA disconnects from a call, (c) the length of breaks taken by the CA, and (d) how frequently the CA requests a team. The VRS provider can use each of these items to assess the amount of time CAs are at their stations and logged in to the system (and thus, able to produce billable minutes for the provider). Billable minutes refers to the number of minutes that a CA is connected to both a deaf and a hearing caller. Only billable minutes can be submitted to the Federal Communications Commission (FCC) for reimbursement to the VRS provider.

Throughout interviews, a commonly expressed reason for why CAs adhere to their providers' expectations was to obtain their desired shift schedule. Participants explained that efficiency reports were used to determine their rank in call centers, which affected their ability to obtain their preferred work schedule. The use of efficiency reports by management impacted the decisions that CAs made both within individual calls as well as outside of calls. This is shown in participants' comments that they often abided by rules simply to increase their chances of obtaining their desired schedule and avoid potential repercussions from management (e.g., losing hours of work, losing their job). However, CAs did show overt resistance to rules when they were determined not to be in the best interest of the caller or themselves. For example, CAs would decide to take an extended break after a particularly difficult call, even if it was not their designated break time. In addition, CAs showed resistance to being shown their efficiency reports on a frequent basis. For example, Carlos David,[1] who had been working in VRS for nearly 10 years, became angry when his provider told him that he could improve his efficiency report by making simple adjustments to his workstation habits. Specifically, Carlos David was advised by his manager that his efficiency reports would improve if he simply moved his water closer in his workstation so that it would be less of a reach. Carlos David perceived his provider's suggestion as micromanagement; however, the impact of his actions on his efficiency report had real-world impact on his ability to obtain future work. He recalled a time when his call center manager wandered through the center with a calculator to show each CA ways to improve efficiency. Carlos David also expressed that he felt he could not behave in a manner that did not align with his beliefs regarding work and personal care. He stated that if the VRS provider was closely monitoring his use of time, he would watch his minutes just as carefully. Further, he stated that he would be careful not to "donate" anything back to the company by shortening his break time, an act of passive resistance.

Similarly to Carlos David, Millie reported that her decisions were often influenced by her desire to obtain future work. She emphasized that she was not alone in her thinking and had noticed this trend in her call center:

> Shifts [are] awarded based on a number of criteria, one being your stats—how quickly you answer the phones. I see interpreters getting right on the phones so they can improve their stats because they have a better chance of getting the shifts that they want.

---

1. All participant names are pseudonyms chosen by the participants to represent themselves in discussion of their interview.

Katie also referenced her log-in percentage in association with her decision to take breaks. She stated,

> We have people who are consistently logged-in to the system during core hours, when it's supposed to be 80% log-in, they are consistently at 90%. Somewhere around there because their perception is "I need the schedule that I want" and so their billable—I mean their interpreting is way too much and of course the company's not going to say a word because they want the billable and if somebody hurts themselves, well you know they shouldn't work in VRS anymore.

Katie's reference to 80% log-in refers to the amount of time she was logged into her call routing software and ready to accept calls. The provider for whom she worked expected that CAs should be sitting in their cubicle and logged in to the computer 80% of their shift. Katie's provider mandated that she take a break for 10 minutes each hour; however, she had noticed that CAs in her center did not take breaks frequently. Instead, they remained logged in to their computer and continued to take calls with the hope of increasing their ranking and, subsequently, the likelihood of obtaining desirable VRS shifts. Skipping breaks may result in successfully obtaining work; however, it most likely also leads to an increased number of errors in interpretation due to exhaustion. Similar to Katie, Millie expressed that efficiency statistics were monitored and used by the VRS schedulers in her call center to determine scheduling priority.

Much like Katie and Millie, Rose noticed that the use of efficiency reports influenced the decisions of CAs in her center. She said CAs often decided not to call in sick or take time off of work to attend family events or for other reasons. Rose admitted that she closely monitored her own statistics in order to make sure that she achieved a priority ranking slot that allowed her to choose her preferred shifts at work. She said,

> I make sure that I check my numbers as often as I can because my numbers have to do with my [schedule] booking rank. Am I able to work based on my numbers? I make a lot of decisions based on that. I have driven to work in dangerous weather conditions because I thought that if I didn't go to work the world would come to an end.

Rose's consistent monitoring of her numbers, as well as her fear of missing a shift even if it were due to uncontrollable weather conditions, suggests the limited professional autonomy she had in her work. Following Sandstrom's (2007) definition of professional autonomy as the ability to use training, reason, and ethics to guide one's own actions, unlike a decision driven by reason and ethics, Rose's decisions were being motivated by the sense of urgency the VRS provider created regarding the scheduling of shifts. Witter-Merithew et al. (2010) assert that autonomy is "achieved when the social conditions that support it are in place and give the practitioner—and consumers—the confidence to take charge of choices" (p. 56). CAs in Rose's center were shown their efficiency statistics as a weekly report, which led to anxiety surrounding their actions and decision-making. Rose, for example, confessed to driving in dangerous weather conditions in order to avoid cancelling a shift. Although she recognized that cancelling a single shift due to inclement weather would not necessarily downgrade her priority ranking, the potential impact was stressful for Rose and led to her decision to brave the weather and go to work.

Throughout the interviews, the participants reported that stress associated with efficiency reports and priority ranking influenced their decision making at work; nevertheless, participants reported that, on occasion, they disregarded rules. The rule that CAs most frequently claimed to disregard was the FCC regulation that a CA should stay with a caller for a minimum of 10 minutes before switching to another CA.[2] In fact, 45% of the participants reported that they had transferred a call prior to the 10-minute regulation. They gave the following reasons: (a) the caller asks to be transferred, (b) the caller is abusive toward the interpreter, (c) the quality of the video is poor, (d) the interpreter cannot stay late, and (e) a team is not available within the center but a team is needed for the call.

Katie referenced a call in which the deaf caller was behaving in a way that she considered abusive:

> There's the 10-minute rule and the FCC bent enough to say that it's the provider's decision to make allowance and they can make a decision. But the problem is they're not sitting there with me and so they can't say, "yes you can switch this call" or "no you can't." That's a decision that I make.

Katie's comment indicated once again that she did not perceive herself as drawing on professional autonomy to make this decision, but rather, she spoke of her actions as a deviation from her provider's expectations.

---

2. This rule has been disputed by some individuals (e.g., Danny Maffia, https://www.streetleverage.com/2015/10/can-clarity-return-discretion-to-vrs-interpreters-repertoire/).

Katie was 59 years old at the time of meeting, had been working as a CA for 10 years, and was heavily involved in efforts to organize a union of CAs in VRS. Due to her involvement in negotiating change in the industry, she was aware that the FCC granted VRS providers the ability to determine whether a CA's action to transfer a VRS call was appropriate; however, she suggested that the provider for whom she worked continued to expect CAs to remain on a call for 10 minutes. Her perspective of deviating from her provider's expectations is not expressed as a reflection of her professional autonomy, and yet, her actions suggest that she is acting in an autonomous manner.

Another interpreter, Cailin, 30 years old at the time of our meeting, explained that switching to a different CA could benefit both the CA and the consumers. She said,

> I'm going to do what I need to do. I'll usually try to make it to the 10 minutes but there's sometimes when I'm just not gonna make it to the 10 minutes. But sometimes what I'll do is maybe call a team and they'll sit down with the person because then it's more smooth for that person and then I'll go sit in their station. . . . I know we're not supposed to hand it off before 10 minutes, but sometimes that's not in the consumer's best interest and it's not in my best interest. Um, sometimes I'll make it to eight or whatever and be like "that's close enough." I'm an ethical interpreter and this is not in your best interest as the consumer. And I know my feelings or attitude are affecting the call. I can't interpret for you.

The decision to exercise professional autonomy by calling a team and then removing herself from the call is an example of an action taken during a VRS call that deviates from provider protocol. The provider for whom Cailin works mandates that CAs remain on a call for a minimum of 10 minutes. Braverman (1998) suggests that bureaucracies often attempt to minimize independent thought and decision making by instituting policies, which are framed as being necessary to ensure the success of the company. Cailin was aware that her provider would not approve of her decision to remove herself from the call; however, in this situation, she referred to herself as "an ethical interpreter" and chose to prioritize customer service and her personal well-being over the stated guidelines. Professional autonomy is reflected in decisions that independent practitioners make about the outcomes of their work that are based on expertise, while also recognizing the system in which one must operate.

Regardless of whether CAs abide by or disregard the rules that govern their work, they are aware of and consider the rules in their decision making. Throughout the interviews, it became clear that most VRS providers consistently used efficiency reports as a management tool, ultimately impacting the ability of CAs to obtain their desired schedule of shifts. Participants disclosed that the manner in which their efficiency reports are shared with them has changed over time. Historically, efficiency reports were posted on the wall of the call center and all employees could see how their efficiency compared with that of their colleagues. Later, pseudonyms were used so that statistics could be compared but the identity of each CA was anonymous. Finally, efficiency reports began being shared via email. Although this method of communication was more private, the impact that the reports had on the professional autonomy of CAs remained consistent.

Interview data revealed that the largest VRS provider routinely shared efficiency reports with CAs; however, one of the smaller VRS providers did not use efficiency reports as a management tool. Employees of this provider expressed that the provider did track CA work statistics, but it was their company's policy not to share these numbers with the CAs. Louise, who was 30 years old at the time of our meeting and had worked with this company for 1 year, said that her manager's philosophy was, "If you don't hear from me then you're doing a good job." Regardless, Louise made sure that she logged in to the computer on time and that she did not take excessively long breaks. She added that there was a book used to log instances that may deviate from the provider's expectations. The fact that there was a book used for this purpose indicates that the provider had rules regarding CAs' work and that CAs were aware their work was monitored. For example, if Louise was called by another CA to work as a team on a call for an extended period of time, she would log the instance in the book; therefore, if her numbers deviated from her provider's expectations, a record existed of what she was doing during the time she was not logged in to her computer. Louise's actions showed that even though the manager did not disclose her statistics, simply knowing that the numbers were tracked by managers still served to constrain CAs' autonomy. Tracking of CA work influenced her decision to log in on time, reduce her break times, and log any deviations from the provider's expectations.

A manager for this smaller VRS provider, Levi, stated, "Numbers are not important," and expressed pride that the provider for whom he works did not focus on numbers. He shared his view that removing the pressure of numbers allowed CAs to focus on customer service. Levi said,

> Yup, we notice that when you look at numbers, um, let's say that you and I are working in the same center and I answer my call in 4 seconds and you answered your call in 6 seconds, how does that affect the customer? It doesn't really. Or how does it affect if the customer wants to give you pre-information before the call to make the call go smoother than it would, so you spend an extra two minutes on them—on that call, building the rapport, getting the information that you needed, making it a very clear partnership type of phone call. That customer is gonna use us again and again in the long run.

Levi said that, as a manager, he is required to track numbers associated with efficiency reports; however, as with Louise's call center, he does not share numbers with CAs unless they deviate from his expectations. During our conversation, Levi pointed out that he only contacts "the outliers" that are evident by his reports. In those instances, he would speak with the CA about the ways in which his or her numbers differ from the call center's standard and discuss ways to get the CA back on track (e.g., timely arrival to shift, shorter breaks).

Joy, who worked for the same provider at a different center, shared that she chose to work for the provider based on their philosophy that they would not share efficiency reports with employees. She had worked as a CA in VRS for 9 months and had never seen her numbers. Similarly, Columbine, who had worked as a CA for 6 months for this provider (also at a different center), had never seen a report of her productivity as compared to her colleagues. She said that if her managers saw a pattern in her numbers over time, they would alert her of their concerns, but so far, no manager had contacted her. When asked if she knew of anyone who had been approached by a manager due to concerns regarding their numbers, Joy responded that she had heard that some of her colleagues had been spoken to about calling for a team too often, but she did not know what resulted from those conversations.

Interviews with the 20 participants in this study showed that CAs were aware that efficiency reports were used to monitor their work. Regardless of whether the results of these reports were shared with them, CAs knew that their work was tracked by management and that there might be penalties for deviating from their provider's expectations of their productivity. CAs working for providers that shared efficiency reports periodically knew that the report would impact their ability to acquire their preferred schedule of work. CAs who worked for providers that did not share efficiency reports were still influenced by the awareness that management tracked their efficiency. They expressed that while they appreciated not being shown their reports, they continued to perceive their autonomy as limited, knowing that the reports existed and could be easily found and reviewed by their provider. In response, CAs would often log their hours or avoid deviating from management's expectations of their efficiency in order to prevent future concerns regarding their work. In sum, management's tracking of CAs' work and use of efficiency reports as a management tool served as limitations to the professional autonomy of CAs.

With the goal of securing future work, CAs follow rules they know will appear on their efficiency report (e.g., break schedule, requesting a team); however, CAs also exercise professional autonomy when they feel it is necessary. Results of this study suggest that CAs exercise professional autonomy in the following four ways: (a) altering their schedule (55%),[3] (b) taking action in response to abusive callers (60%), (c) calling for a team (50%), and (d) modeling realistic expectations of performance (e.g., log-in time, breaks) (20%). These actions are taken in response to the theme of tracking of CA work.

PURPOSEFUL SCHEDULING

Participants expressed that adhering to management's strict expectations of productivity resulted in elevated levels of stress. For this reason, CAs perceived that their autonomy to care for their own well-being during their scheduled VRS shift was severely limited. As a result, actions of professional autonomy were evidenced outside of VRS calls. CAs exercised professional autonomy regarding the shifts that they chose to work (i.e., weekday vs. weekend, day vs. night), as well as the length of their shifts and breaks. Of the 20 interpreters interviewed, 11 (55%) expressed that they purposefully planned their shifts in order to care for their own

---

3. Given the small sample size of this study ($n = 20$), percentages are offered in order to offer perspective to the number of participants who have taken a particular action. In addition, there may be some overlap in cases where a participant referenced more than one action (e.g., alter schedule and calling for a team).

well-being. They perceived that they did not have the autonomy to take breaks when needed due to management's tracking of their productivity. In order to reduce stress, CAs scheduled lengthy breaks, worked specific shifts in response to call volume, and reduced the number of consecutive work hours. As previously mentioned, percentages reflect only those instances in which the topic was present during the course of discussion. Lack of discussion among the remaining 45% of participants does not necessarily signify a different strategy (or the same strategy) used by interpreters, but rather that the discussion was not raised. Although participants introduced topics regarding a number of influencing factors on their decisions about breaks and shift selection, the major causal factor was stress associated with management's tracking of their work.

Tux, who had been a CA for 8 years, expressed that the job was extraordinarily stressful. She emphasized her preference to work in the morning for two reasons. First, she had family responsibilities that required her to be home in the afternoons. Second, she paid close attention to the company's tracking of her efficiency statistics (e.g., time, teaming, billable minutes) and had chosen to work only morning shifts. For the provider with whom Tux worked, expectations of efficiency differed depending on the time of the shift. In the mornings, interpreters were expected to be logged in to the provider's software and ready to accept calls 80% of their shift, with the remaining time allotted for breaks at a rate of 10 minutes of break time for each hour of work. After 6:00 p.m., interpreters were expected to be logged in 85% of their shift time due to increased workload resulting from fewer CAs scheduled to work in the evenings. In reference to the choices regarding her schedule, Tux said,

> I work in the mornings because my kids go to school, so I like to be home when they are home. Um, one reason why I wouldn't like to work in the afternoons is because login would be 85% so then you are expected to be sitting even longer. And nobody likes that. Because supposedly call volume is less so you are expected to be logged in longer so that you have a higher chance of getting phone calls. It's tougher and you would get less breaks.

Tux admitted that she needed to be a mathematician to be an effective CA according to her company's standards:

> We have numbers on the screen like available minutes—the log-in minutes, you know how long I've been there waiting for a phone call. And

it will tell me my billable minutes [how long I am connected to both a hearing and deaf caller]. Then we have a matrix that tells me, "if you're working two hours, this is how many minutes 50% would be. If you're working 2 hours, this is what 80% log-in would be." One thing I always say is that if you're going to come to VRS interpreting, you must be good at math. It sounds funny, but it's true. You need to know because then, especially if you work part of the morning, but then you pass 6:00 p.m. Passing 6:00 p.m. is 85%. You need to know math.

Tux pointed out that the time of day was a factor that influenced her decision to take a break because her provider's expectation of the percentage of time she was logged in to the computer and ready to take calls changed after 6:00 p.m. The change in expectations would be noted in her efficiency report and could potentially impact her ability to reserve future preferred hours of work.

Bella, who had worked as a CA for 10 years, blamed the rules governing the work of CAs in the VRS setting for her exhaustion. She specifically referenced a time when her provider changed the method and frequency in which efficiency reports were shared with CAs. Since this change, Bella had become more mindful of the length of her breaks. In the past, her report and the efficiency reports of other CAs were posted on the wall of the call center using pseudonyms. Efficiency reports then began to be shared more frequently using email. Given the constant reminder of her efficiency, Bella shortened the length of her shifts in VRS. She said,

> I used to not care about breaks, if it was 12 minutes it was 12 minutes, but they show you your numbers constantly. So I shortened my shifts, I've adjusted myself to their rules. Unfortunately, we're always behind as a field to get our own needs known. FCC set up their rules, they didn't know our needs, and now we're all struggling with this. And maybe it will all [change] seriously in 20 years, seriously when everybody finally complains enough and everybody finally gets on the same page. That's 20 to 30 years to me. So now, if that's how these companies have to stay in business, then I'm gonna shorten my hours and that's all I have, so if I shorten my hours and I can't come to you as much and you don't have enough interpreters, then you're gonna beg the FCC to change these rules. But how long is that gonna take?

Bella stated that the regulations set forth by the FCC were the driving force behind her decision to reduce her hours; however, the FCC does not establish rules regarding break times. Rules regarding breaks are established by VRS providers. Bella showed passive resistance in her approach to her schedule, assuming that it would take decades for the FCC to change its rules. She viewed the rules associated with providers as being established in compliance with FCC regulations and blames the FCC for her exhaustion. By associating her break schedule with the FCC, Bella perceived that she did not have the power to use her own reason and ethics to make decisions regarding her ability to do the work. Instead, she reported that her only option for expressing her disfavor of these regulations was to reduce her hours. She further stated that she hoped the provider would notice that the seasoned interpreters in the field were not willing to work under the current stressful conditions.

Levi, who had worked in VRS for 12 years and was a manager at the time of the interview, exercised professional autonomy by incorporating longer breaks into the planning of his shifts. Given his managerial position, Levi had more professional autonomy (and therefore control over his shift) than his colleagues who were strictly CAs without managerial responsibilities. He shared,

> I get here about 8:00 in the morning, and then I work usually peak hours. You know 8:00–5:00. Personally, I take about an hour break in the middle of that time just to step away. I found that a half hour for myself wasn't quite long enough so an hour is a good time to sit down and eat and then I still have about a half hour to go. We have a library right down the road here so I usually walk down to the library for a little bit, sit and read a magazine and then I walk back.

The provider with whom Levi worked offered a 30-minute lunch break for a full day of work. In fact, the norm is 30 minutes in VRS work, as reported by the participants who worked for a variety of providers. However, Levi commented that, for him, a 30-minute break was insufficient to resolve the fatigue associated with VRS work. He determined that he was more mentally prepared for VRS when he incorporated an extended break into his schedule. During this unpaid break, he preferred to detach entirely from work by leaving the call center and walking to the library.

Similarly, Cailin, who had worked as a CA for the past 5 years, also made the decision to include extended breaks into her schedule. The provider that she worked for allowed a 10-minute break each hour; however, Cailin expressed that she needed a longer break in order to be able to continue to be mentally prepared to interpret. She said,

I had a 3-hour limit. I would [interpret] 3 hours, half-hour break, un-paid, and then 3 hours, half-hour break unpaid, and then 3 hours. I purposely did that so that no matter how busy it was, I would have 30 minutes where I didn't have to worry about it . . . I had a break. So that at . . . any point of exhaustion or any point of "oh my God (scratches at eyes)," I was two hours away from a break. And it really helped me mentally. That's the only way I'll do it now.

Cailin discussed the notion of burnout at length during our discussion. She reported that her exhaustion was not fair to either the callers or her-self. She said,

That's partially why I have taken a step back [from VRS], why I have inserted the breaks, because I noticed I wasn't interpreting to my full ability. I want every time I interpret for the person to have the best that I can do. I know that I do not do that towards the end of the day. I just don't. And at the end of the day, this is going to sound horrible, I don't care at the end of the day. I'm so tired and I'm so worn out.

Incorporating planned breaks into her schedule is evidence of Cailin's perception that she did not have the freedom to decide when she needed a break during her VRS shift. Identifying her limited autonomy, Cailin determined that she needed to insert lengthy breaks outside of her assigned shift, allowing her to continue to serve each caller to the best of her ability while managing her fatigue at the same time. Sandstrom (2007) suggests that limitations to professional autonomy are common in capitalist production where human decision making is perceived as a threat to standardization and profit. A common response to perceived limitations among CAs was the establishment of a predetermined, fixed break schedule in order to exercise self-care.

In addition, interviews showed that participants purposefully chose to work particular shifts in an effort to practice self-care. Katie, who was 59 years old at the time of our interview, had worked as a CA for 10 years. She said,

An accommodation that I make for myself is that I work weekends and evenings because the pace is typically slower, not always but, you know. I think you have fewer hours that are as intense as they are in what [the company] calls their "core hours."

Katie's reasons for selecting her shift differed from those of Holly, a younger interpreter who had worked in VRS for 4 years. Holly expressed that she refused to work night shifts because she could not be sure that a team would be available given that there were fewer CAs scheduled. Providers often schedule fewer CAs in the late night or early morning hours when businesses are closed and many people are sleeping. Given the reduced rate of incoming calls, providers have determined that fewer CAs are needed. Given the understanding that the provider for whom she worked expected that she not transfer calls outside of the center, Holly made the decision to avoid night shifts so that there was a greater chance that a team would be available should she need assistance during a call.

Similarly, Tux expressed that the stress associated with VRS created an environment that was not conducive to continuous employment. She stated that she felt confined to her booth given the extent to which her provider tracked her time. She worried about her ability to obtain future work based on her productivity and felt limited in her break schedule. Throughout our discussion, Tux continuously returned to the topic of stress. She said that she did not have time to talk to her colleagues, relax, or even use the restroom. She continued,

> I love my job, but it is very stressful. It's a stressful job. It's not for everybody either. It might not be for someone for the rest of their life. Maybe do it part time or maybe do it for a couple years and then go somewhere else.

Tux was not alone in her feelings of anxiety associated with her VRS work. Although data from this study suggest that CAs make decisions to alter their schedule for a number of reasons, a recurring finding is that stress and the goal of self-care are major influences on the decision to implement schedule changes. The CAs simply did not perceive that they could make decisions during their scheduled VRS shift given that each decision they made could be easily tracked and may impact their ability to secure future work.

TAKING ACTION IN RESPONSE TO ABUSIVE CALLERS

During the course of this study, participants often discussed the stress that they felt in reference to callers that they considered abusive toward them and the influence these abusive situations had on their decisions regarding the work. Participants expressed that VRS providers have protocols regarding CAs' actions in response to calls they perceive as abusive (e.g., submitting a report of the incident to a manager). CAs are expected to follow the designated protocol, which may include documentation of various details regarding the incident (e.g., time of call, phone number of caller).

Although CAs are located at a physical distance from their callers and are often unfamiliar to the callers they work with, they experience abuse in a variety of forms. In a study of CA burnout, Bower (2013) notes the stressors VRS CAs felt in association with their work. Abusive stressors include sexually explicit remarks directed toward the CA and callers who expose themselves physically to the CA. Additional abuse can be seen in harsh or harmful comments made toward the CA (e.g., lousy interpreter, stupid interpreter). At this writing, no research has been done on the experience of abuse by CAs. Without the ability to observe VRS calls, any research would be self-reported and retrospective. Regardless of the type of abuse, VRS providers have specific protocols that they expect CAs to follow in response to callers they perceive as abusive. If protocols are not followed, CAs' actions may be misconstrued in the provider's tracking of productivity. For example, a CA may receive a call from the same abusive caller several times during a late-night VRS shift when fewer CAs are working or repeatedly over the course of several days. If the CA refuses to accept calls from this caller, without reporting the incidences using proper provider protocol, the CA's actions may be perceived as refusing service to a deaf caller or, from a quantitative standpoint, poor productivity.

In response to a situation the CA considers abusive, provider protocol states the CA may submit a formal complaint to the VRS provider about a deaf caller for inappropriate behavior (e.g., caller is naked, sexual comments to the interpreter). Aside from formal complaints, 60% of the participants expressed that they also took further measures to keep record of instances they perceived could lead the provider to pursue disciplinary action against them (e.g., the caller threatens to report the CA to the VRS provider). Although participants were not sure what disciplinary actions would be taken in regard to these situations, they were aware that their provider tracks incidences when a caller reports a CA.

Given the interpersonal nature of interpreting work, it is not surprising that complications arise with consumers on occasion. For reasons pertaining to customer service, most of the participants expressed that when a deaf caller seemed angry with the CA, their first attempt to remedy the situation occurred within the call. CAs often decided to work directly with a caller to solve the problem (e.g., asking for clarification, apologizing for perceived concerns with interpretation). CAs attempted to demonstrate visible qualities of customer service (e.g., smiling) and show empathy with the caller. Managing feelings to create a publicly observable display has been considered a type of emotional labor (Hochschild, 1983). Throughout the study of CAs, the notions of "killing them [callers] with kindness," "trying to put myself in their shoes," and "answering every call with a smile on my face" were raised by several participants. Regardless, if resolution with the caller could not be achieved, the next step was often to offer to switch the caller to another CA (either internally within the call center or externally to another call center). Participants expressed that sometimes removing themselves from the situation was enough to satisfy the caller. Finally, participants who perceived that a caller might file a complaint against them expressed that they actively sought out their manager for support. Confiding in a manager served two purposes: (a) the manager would be aware of the potential complaint before it arrived and could support the CA's decisions if the complaint was actually brought to their attention, and (b) the manager was often a colleague with CA experience who could emotionally support the CA after a situation that the CA perceived was abusive.

In addition, some CAs made personal notes about the situation in a log that they kept in their personal notebook or online calendar. The notes described by CAs did not contain personal information (e.g., names, phone numbers), but rather situational clues (e.g., language used, actions taken) that could serve as a reminder of the situation if a concern was brought to their attention (e.g., complaint made by caller, provider investigation of abusive caller). Given the constant monitoring of CA work, CAs appeared to be conditioned to take measures to protect themselves from management's oversight and possible disciplinary actions. This may be due to the ease with which a complaint can be filed against a CA. Complaints can be made simply via email or videophone call to the VRS provider; no further action is necessary. The complaint process in VRS drastically differs from complaints made to the Registry of Interpreters for the Deaf (RID) regarding interpreters outside of VRS, which reflects a "multi-level grievance system" (RID, 2015b). Individuals who file a complaint are expected to participate in mediation. This requires a great deal more effort on the part of the complainant. Findings from the study of CAs indicate that CAs apply strategies to protect themselves from complaints made by consumers. Regardless of the type of information the CA maintains after a call or the intent of the CA, retaining information can be considered a violation of Section 225 of the Americans With Disabilities Act (1990), which prohibits CAs from "disclosing the content of any relayed conversation and from keeping records of the content of any such conversation beyond the duration of the call."

Rose, who had been working in VRS for the past 7 years, expressed that when callers showed signs of anger she first assessed whether they were disgruntled with the person whom they were calling or with herself as the CA. Aside from the mental energy required to perform an interpretation, Rose was exerting additional energy to assess the emotions of the caller and determine her actions in response to the caller's concerns. Rose emphasized that it was important not to internalize anger that was not directed toward her. If she determined that the anger being expressed via profane language or harsh expression was directed toward her, she would then communicate with callers in order to resolve any concerns. During our interview, Rose said,

> Well, most times my first question is "I understand you don't like what I did. I can change what I'm doing and try to work with you or I can transfer you to another interpreter. What are you more comfortable with?" And I put it right back on them. "I understand that I have done something that has upset you. I can change it or I can't change it and this is why I can't change it."

Rose's actions indicate that she was willing to work directly with the caller to resolve the problem, but if she could not resolve the issue for any reason, she would explain to the caller what rules were in place that kept her from complying with their request. During our discussion, Rose emphasized that she finds that callers appreciate "transparency." They want to know what she is doing and what she claims she cannot do in reference to her service. For this reason, she prefers to be candid with the caller and communicate exactly what she was doing and how it either could or could not change. If she decided that she could not change her actions and this was unacceptable to the caller, Rose would then transfer the call to a new CA. Although this seems like a mutually agreed upon next step, it is worth mentioning that transferring the caller to a new CA would appear in reports of CA productivity. In addition, the act of transferring the call would place the caller back in queue to wait for an available CA and then require the caller to begin his or her call all over again. Brunson (2010) refers to this as *calculated consumer labor*. The caller "must determine the benefits and drawbacks of doing (or not doing) a particular activity" (Brunson, 2010, p. 2), in this case either continuing with the call or requesting a new CA and starting the process all over again.

Similarly, Louise expressed that she did not take offense when a caller requested a different interpreter. She said, "I always tell them that I am more than happy to transfer them to another interpreter. It doesn't bother me. I don't get offended by it." Louise had been working as a CA for 1 year at the time of our interview. She seemed to be aware that in some instances the caller might be happier with a different CA. Another participant, Dr. S, who had been working as a CA for nearly 8 years, expressed that CAs who "have been [working in VRS] the longest are, uh a little bit more, I guess I would call it leathery (laughs). We kind of let things roll off a little bit more." The notions of needing "thick skin" in VRS or "letting problems/insults roll off your back" were raised by several of the participants. An ability to not take things personally seems to be an important characteristic to combat the stress that arises while working in VRS.

Riley, a seasoned CA, expressed that she never offered to transfer callers to a new CA. She felt that if she didn't understand the caller with her 12 years of experience, then most likely whomever she transferred the caller to would struggle as well. After making this statement, Riley paused for a moment and said that she would like to change her response. She said,

> There was a time when I was new at this—12 years ago—if they said they didn't want me I was like (DEFLATE),[4] like my whole world was you know crushed. I don't feel that way anymore. You know? I've been doing this for too long and I know I'm not a match for everybody. If I think they are getting all riled up because of me, I will say "do you want me to switch you to another interpreter?"

Riley's approach was to evaluate whether the caller's frustrations were based on her as the CA or due to other factors. If she determined that she was the cause of the problem, she would offer to transfer to another CA. As Brunson (2010) points out, the caller must determine whether the benefits of receiving the service outweigh the emotional cost required to

---

4. Instances where interpreters expressed themselves using American Sign Language during interviews are glossed and expressed in small capital letters throughout this text.

get the service (i.e., being placed back in queue for a new interpreter and reinitiating the call process).

CAs preferred to practice their professional autonomy to resolve concerns independently; however, they were prepared to take further action in response to the provider's system under which they work if needed. Levi, who had worked for a small provider for 12 years, expressed that he often saw the same deaf callers repeatedly. In analyzing Levi's transcript, it became apparent that he had a strong relationship with his callers and he wanted to offer them quality interpreting service to the best of his ability. Levi also discussed a few instances involving callers whose actions he determined to be unacceptable. Although he preferred not to report these callers, he identified some situations where the only plausible action was to disconnect from the call and make a report. He shared,

> I would say I have a pretty tough skin so I can take a lot before there's that line where I have to disconnect. With that caller, that line has probably been pushed back towards them a little bit more. Since you know what this has been happening forever. But you know there are callers that it's the first time that I'm experiencing this and I give them a little more leeway. Like I said, it could have been a horrible day and this is just where it's coming up. I feel comfortable when I do disconnect because I've given them warning. I've given them the reason that I would disconnect. I've given them options to modify their behavior before I disconnect.

Levi explained that his decision to disconnect and report one particular caller was driven by the fact that it was not the first time that the problem had arisen. He had spoken to the caller before about similar concerns. After attempting to reconcile the situation directly with the caller, Levi was ready with a back-up strategy. His company's policy was that each time a CA disconnected from a caller, a formal report of the situation needed to take place. The provider kept this record in case the FCC raised concerns regarding the interpreter's actions. In addition, as a manager, Levi noted that when other CAs took similar actions to those he had taken in disconnecting the call, he used the documentation of the incident to follow up with the CA. Levi said,

> As a manager sometimes I use those documentations also to go and pull the interpreter off the phone and just talk about that. "O.K., this is the way that you approached that call. And the reason that you

disconnected it. So let's talk about the positives and negatives for the way that you did it. Now let's try to explore other ways that you possibly could have handled that call."

For the provider Levi worked for, reporting a caller's actions may call into question the actions of the CA as well. In an effort to avoid being called to a manager's office and asked to justify their actions, CAs may avoid reporting callers or, in some cases, decide to maintain their own personal record of an incident instead of using provider protocols. As previously mentioned, this action is prohibited by FCC regulations.

CAs reported keeping records of situations independently (as opposed to within the company system) for their own protection. After interpreting for a caller who she suspected would submit a complaint, Riley said,

> I'll put it [in my calendar] on the date that it happened so in case something comes up later I can look back and remind myself. I just wanna make sure that I can remember what happened, why I did what I did. I make sure that my manager is aware of it the moment that it happened.

Riley referred to her practices as a "CYA [cover your ass] thing." She took these actions in order to ensure that she would not experience disciplinary action from her company. She made no reference to whether she maintained these types of records for a specific period of time before deleting them or whether they were permanent additions to her calendar.

Riley had worked as a CA for three different providers and was not alone in her actions. Other CAs expressed that they frequently took action if they were concerned that disciplinary action may be taken against them. Red, who was 27 years old at the time of our interview, had been working as a CA for 7 years. He shared that he proactively responded to the risk of disciplinary action by always calling a team when he had concerns that a complaint might be made in regard to his work. He said,

> If it comes down to [needing] to talk about this with a manager I can say, "such and such was on the call too and they saw me do the right thing," or whatever. So there's a CYA element to calling a team.

Throughout this study, calling for a team was often referred to as having "a second pair of eyes" on the call. Red expressed using this backup as a form of protection if a caller chose to complain about the service he provided, despite the fact that calling for a team frequently is frowned upon by VRS providers and would appear on reports of CA productivity. Participants also reported that it was not uncommon for deaf consumers of VRS to threaten to report a CA. The consumers did not always follow through with these threats; however, once the threat had been made, some CAs expressed the need to take steps to protect themselves.

For example, one deaf consumer told Sharon, who had been working as a CA for almost 10 years, that he planned to report her behavior to the provider. She expressed that because the threat was made, she wanted to make sure that she also shared her side of the story:

> He didn't report me, [but] because I was waiting, I told my manager, I was like, "This is what happened, if you get a complaint then this is my side of the story," which is probably helpful to have. I think it is important that you get your side of the story because you get so many calls that [by the time it comes up again] you don't remember.

Another CA, Jill, said that she preferred to keep a record of these situations by sending an email to her manager. She mentioned that the manager preferred to receive identifying information such as the time of the call, the phone number of the caller, and an IP address if one was available; however, Jill often just noted the time of the call because she knew that the company could find more information if it wanted to investigate further. Aside from the initial information, Jill explained,

> I would probably just bullet point like the series of events that happened. Like you know, "initiated call, caller wasn't happy with call or unhappy with tech problems." Um, or yeah like what did I feel, from like my perspective, was their issue. Um, or was there anything directed toward me. I wrote down like what I saw, what I felt, and then I just said "this is what happened." I don't know if she's gonna like write me up, but it was kinda just being proactive.

Other CAs noted that they had reported abusive callers not necessarily because they were personally offended by a caller's actions, but rather because they wanted to protect their colleagues, even those whom they had never met, from having a similar challenging experience. They expressed that they reported callers in hopes that the VRS provider would take action. Red wished that callers had a way of formally indicating through a provider that they did not want to work with a specific CA. With this type of mechanism in place, their call would not be routed to the CA at all. Red went on to say that he always removes himself from situations in which the caller is abusive and fills out a detailed report through the provider's established protocol. He said,

> Any time that the attention shifts towards me in a negative way it's pretty much immediate grounds for me to recuse for the rest of the call. Because I mean especially if it's coming in a very angry way. Um, I mean a lot. If they're just saying "Ugh, I just told you. What's this (random sign)? I don't know that sign." and you're like, I can negotiate all day. But as soon as [they're] like "terrible interpreter" I'm like . . . nothing from now on is gonna go the way it should, so let's just get you someone else. I'll even get a team and switch out and still support you since I know the context.

Participants frequently discussed the ways they protected themselves from the complaints submitted by callers. They knew that management kept records of this information and would make them aware of each complaint submitted regarding their work. However, they did not perceive their own complaints about the actions of deaf callers being addressed in the same manner. Red said that he didn't think that the provider responded to all complaints submitted by CAs. He said,

> It has to reach a critical mass before any action gets taken. But that's why I'm pretty diligent to do it, because if it's happening to me, it's happening to every interpreter they interact with. I protect them that way as well. My feelings don't get hurt too easily but I also say "if I don't report it you're going to continue and it's gonna happen with other interpreters." We can't have that.

Red had worked for two different providers over the past 7 years. After hearing that I was looking for male participants for my study, he recommended that I speak with his colleague, Carlos David. Carlos David had been working for the same provider for 10 years. He shared,

> It's not necessarily harassment to me, because I can deflect those pretty well. But you're just an overall rude angry person and, especially like in the nighttime or early morning hours, there's only like five of us working so we each get it maybe three or four times during a night. And you're rude about it. You just need to go to bed, relax, put the beer down, and stop calling. But hey it's your right to call. I get that. But I would also like to make a note of the time or date or something like this person is way out of control. I believe those get addressed.

Both Red and Carlos David's comments indicated that action would be taken if interpreters report callers repeatedly; however, neither CA reported that they had followed up in regard to these calls. There was no evidence from providers explicating their evaluation of reports of abuse or the subsequent actions taken in response to abusive callers.

Tux also shared two experiences with reporting callers. In the first, the deaf caller appeared on screen but Tux could not see the caller's face. She stated, "I could only see them from the waist down." In the second call, the caller used negative language directed toward the CA. Although Tux did not share the exact words that the caller said, she seemed visibly upset when discussing the incident and said,

> Um, the caller was not being respectful to the interpreter. And also, I knew that they wouldn't be respectful to other interpreters. I knew that there was a history of that. Uh so, I'm not gonna, I'm not gonna take it. Not even one time. And just—I had heard it all around, you know, "talking down" to interpreters. I respect you as the Deaf client and you're gonna respect me as the interpreter. I'm not here for your negative comments.

Tux identified that this was a caller who had repeatedly demonstrated this type of behavior. For this reason, she felt it necessary to report the caller. In general, Tux expressed that she considered herself a "rule follower." Throughout our discussion she referenced provider-initiated rules and how they corresponded to her ability to obtain her desired schedule of VRS shifts. She worked 32 to 34 hours per week in VRS and shared that she was very aware of her responsibilities (as indicated by her efficiency report). She described that she actively treated all callers with respect and, in return, expected them to show respect to her and her colleagues as well.

The interview data revealed that CAs also made professional decisions based on the unity they felt with their colleagues. They did not want their fellow CAs to experience abuse or receive disciplinary action resulting from performance tracking. For example, Dr. S recalled a rule established by her VRS provider stating that CAs are expected to transfer calls only to CAs outside of their call center if the center was closing. If a CA received a call that was transferred to his or her station from a CA at another call center, the CA was mandated to note the transferring CA's identifying number and report the incident to a manager. Dr. S was aware of this provider-initiated rule but confessed to never following this expectation. She said,

If they transfer to another center we're supposed to put down the [interpreter's] number and give it [to our manager]. Um, that's probably a rule that I break because I know that we're all together and so we have enough to deal with with callers and so I will fudge that and I won't tell on an interpreter if they transfer to me. I don't know per se what happened to you, I do know that it would be brought to your attention, um it hasn't ever happened to me. You know, our center manager has said, "if that happens again, you know tell me so that I can contact their center manager and they can address it." But in the back of my head, I'm just like "mmm I'm probably not gonna tell you that" because you know I just have a hard time ratting out a fellow VI [video interpreter].

Dr. S was aware that she was "breaking the rules" by not reporting the CA who transferred the call but expressed a greater sense of alignment with her fellow CAs (even those whom she had never met) as opposed to the VRS provider. She was unsure as to whether reporting the CA would have led to the CA receiving a "slap on the wrist" or being formally written up by the manager, but, regardless, she chose not to report the CA. Throughout our discussion, Dr. S also expressed concern regarding fatigue and burnout. She had worked as a CA for nearly 8 years and frequently referred to the stress associated with VRS work.

MODELING REALISTIC PERFORMANCE EXPECTATIONS

Individual providers, in compliance with FCC regulations, establish expectations of CA performance on the job. For example, the FCC established the expectation that VRS calls should be answered within a certain amount of time (FCC, n.d.). The goal of this expectation is to ensure that deaf callers are receiving functionally equivalent access to telecommunication services, equivalent to the access that hearing people experience when they pick up the phone and hear a dial tone. Reducing the amount of time that deaf people have to wait for access to telecommunication services supports the goal of functional equivalency. Individual VRS providers, however, introduced limits on how many CAs are working at any given time. The employee limit drives down the number of CAs available to accept calls and affects the expectations of CA efficiency. Efficiency is tracked by VRS providers and may be addressed by the providers in varying ways. Some providers track interpreter efficiency through statistics (e.g., log-in time, speed of call answer, speed of hang up after call) to ensure compliance with FCC regulations. During the interviews, 20% of participants stated that their decisions were influenced by the expectations of CA performance.

Holly recalled when she first started working in VRS. She was 24 years old and felt that she was fortunate to be working with some of the best interpreters in her state. Holly was highly motivated to be starting her career in VRS. She was a new interpreter and felt that her new position in VRS offered her the opportunity to become a professional. As Brunson (2011) points out, interpreters who are not yet certified and are considered trainees in the VRS setting still earn considerably more than they would earn if they worked outside of VRS without certification. During our discussion, Holly described her initial excitement at the prospect of working in VRS and her eventual shock when she discovered how some of her colleagues responded to her actions. She said,

> The company that I worked for before would post all the VI stats. When I first started there I was like (MOTIVATE). I just wanna work and I was so grateful and thankful that this company brought me on. I would have interpreters come up to me be like (gestures with hand palm out) "look kid, like look at your—you're logged in 95% of your shift today, like you're bringing us all down. We don't wanna do that but you're setting this precedent way up here and we're, like, no we're lucky if we're gonna get 80%."

It was not Holly's intention to skew the company's perception of her ability to perform at certain levels. She was new to the field and did not realize that her decisions impacted her colleagues. Ever since this outcome was brought to her attention, Holly has carefully considered her decisions and how they may influence the perception of a CA's ability to work extended periods without breaks. Holly now takes 10-minute breaks every hour, even when she does not necessarily feel that a break is needed.

Similarly, Millie reported that she also considers her colleagues when determining her break schedule. Millie was 52 years old at the time of our interview and had worked in VRS for 5 years. She commuted long distance to the call center twice a month and worked 8-hour days. She stated that she enjoyed the camaraderie of working in VRS because there were few interpreters in her rural hometown. Millie noted that her current decisions drastically differ from the decisions she made regarding her work when she first started in VRS. In fact, she noted that her decisions also differed from those of her peers who worked more frequently in VRS. She said,

> Some of the other interpreters are there on a more regular basis and that's their primary gig. Because of the burnout—because of just um being there so often, working so many hours in that situation—I can kinda come in fresh, you know? I haven't been there in a couple weeks . . . and I can blitz. I can work 8-hour days. I can go without breaks. But I realize that's not fair for the other interpreters.

Millie went on to say that, because she did not work frequently, she came in to each shift "excited, enthusiastic, and fresh." Although it would be easy for her to come in and work hard for 8 continuous hours, she kept her colleagues in mind. Millie expressed that she had seen the exhaustion of her colleagues in the break room. She said,

> I see that burnout, I see they're getting tired, I see they're getting frustrated with calls. I mean [I know one interpreter who] can handle any call and when she calls for a team it's usually because she's just so done with—you know she wants to strangle the deaf person and "how can a videophone be given to someone whose so stupid?" type of comments.

As with Holly, Millie understood that even if she did not feel that she needed a break, her failure to take the time would affect the provider's perception of the ability of CAs to work for extended periods of time; therefore, she adhered to the expected pattern of taking breaks throughout her shift. In this way, she expressed an understanding that her actions are monitored by the provider and that, when compiled, this information may contribute to the provider's perception of realistic work expectations.

CAs showed awareness of the need to take breaks for reasons pertaining to self-care; however, they recognized that breaks are tracked by VRS providers and expressed that their decisions also aimed to support the ability of their colleagues to take breaks if needed. Emily, who had been working as a CA for 5 years at the time of our interview, worked for a provider that required CAs to schedule their breaks so that they were not all taking breaks at the same time (thus ensuring CAs were available to answer calls and the provider was able to meet the "speed of answer" requirement set by the FCC while controlling for the number of CAs working at any given time). "Speed of answer" refers to the total number of seconds that a call can wait in queue before connecting to a CA. Emily shared that she did not have the freedom to determine when she could take a break. Instead, if she had a particularly long or stressful call and it was not her turn to take a break, she would send out an internal message to her colleagues using the provider's chat software to ask if she could switch break times with someone. Emily was aware that this decision would impact her colleagues and their ability to take a break; therefore, she tried to do it only when necessary. Similarly, she shared that if she was on hold for a long time (which was often the case with larger businesses and organizations) and therefore not actively interpreting, she would support her colleagues by offering her break to someone else. She said,

> Say for example you are on a long Social Security hold. I mean most of those holds are at least 30 minutes. So, if it's my turn to take a break I might just put an IM out there, whoever is next you know go ahead and jump me [in line] because I'm just sitting here, I'm not really working, so go ahead and jump me.

Columbine, who had worked as a CA for 6 months, also considered her colleagues when deciding to take breaks. The provider she worked for asked that CAs sign up for breaks by adding their name to a list. The CAs then took their breaks in the order in which they had indicated on the list. It was preferred that CAs did not take a break when it was not their designated time in order to prevent several CAs from being off of the phones simultaneously. During our interview Columbine mentioned a particularly long call during which she would have liked to have taken a break but it was not her turn. She said,

> I just did [the call] and then took a break afterward. Breaks are kind of "in turn." So we have a list and once you get to the top of the list you take a break, then you end up on the bottom of the list and it cycles through. So if you need to, you can take a break out of turn. But you wouldn't do that too often. It's just not fair to the others.

CAs expressed that their decisions were often influenced by the efficiency reports used by VRS providers to track CA productivity and their own desire to set an appropriate example of the needs of VRS CAs. In addition, their decisions were influenced by their recognition that working in a VRS setting is stressful and that CAs do not have the freedom to use their professional ethics to guide their actions. Regardless of the constraints placed on professional autonomy, the decisions CAs made often were guided by their desire to care for the well-being of their colleagues.

CALLING FOR A TEAM

CAs in VRS often work independently; however, they may evaluate a VRS call and determine that a second CA is necessary. The RID Standard Practice Paper on team interpreting defines this process as "the utilization of two or more interpreters who support each other to meet the needs of a particular communication situation" (RID, 2007a). Hoza (2010) points out that interpreters who work in community settings often do so in teams. Teaming occurs for a number of reasons including the length of the interaction, its complexity, and the physical or emotional dynamics of the situation. In these situations, two interpreters may collaborate in an effort to ensure the accuracy of the message. Collaboration between interpreters may exist in a number of ways, including monitoring the overall setting, assuring appropriate and timely transitions between interpreters, and supporting other interpreters as needed for the accuracy of the message (RID, 2007a). Hoza (2010) notes, "Team interpreting is now common practice in the field and accounts for approximately 30% of interpreting assignments" (p. 1).

In the VRS setting, providers mandate that a team be present for all 911 calls. When a 911 call appears, a team is automatically notified. Aside from 911 calls, CAs individually evaluate each call and determine whether a team member is necessary. For example, if a CA works during normal business hours (i.e., 9:00 a.m. to 5:00 p.m., with consideration for varying time zones), it is not uncommon to interpret a conference call. A conference call occurs between a group of people as opposed to just two conversational participants. It may last for an extended amount of time. In addition, it may include complex terminology specific to the organization initiating the call. For all of these reasons, CAs often request a team for support with conference calls.

Participants in the study stated that VRS providers expected them to call for team support during lengthy calls or calls during which the CA struggled with comprehension. Providers may have developed this rule in response to the Telecommunications Relay Service Rules (2011), which state that the CA must continue with a call for a minimum of 10 minutes and may not refuse calls. The goal of this rule is to prevent callers from being transferred repetitively to different CAs due to difficult call content, challenging linguistic stimuli, or complex interactions. Delays caused by finding an interpreter willing to accept the call would be a barrier to the notion of functionally equivalent telecommunication service to that experienced by hearing people.

Apart from conference calls and calls in which the CA struggles with understanding (e.g., callers with physical limitations that impact their language production, international callers), 50% of the participants expressed that they assessed each call individually and used their personal ethics to determine their ability to effectively interpret the call. They reported calling a team any time that they perceived it was necessary. In some instances, the perceived need for a team was due to the desire for emotional support (e.g., calls involving serious illness, death, or abuse). In others, the participant noted personal fatigue. CAs were aware that the number of times that they called for a team was information that VRS providers might track and that it could be raised as an issue for the CA in the future; however, they showed little concern that disciplinary actions would be taken. Throughout the interviews, participants mentioned that teaming appeared in their efficiency reports and could impact their ability to choose their shifts. They stated that they had been called to their manager's office to discuss the potential need for additional training. However, not one participant mentioned additional actions taken or having any concern about losing his or her job.

Participants expressed that the use of efficiency reports influenced their decision regarding whether to call for a team to support them in interpreting a call. Refraining from calling a team can impact the quality of the interpretation; however, CAs acknowledged that because the number of times that they called for a team was tracked by management, they were less inclined to call for a team. In addition, they were aware that some of their colleagues had been called to their manager's office and reprimanded for calling a team too often. Riley said,

> The people who are sadly getting in trouble for [calling a team too frequently] are probably the people who really need it because they're new and they need the support. And they're still getting used to everything. I think if somebody talked to me about my numbers I would probably try not to call a team because I'm a rule follower and I'm trying to get my numbers to look the way they're supposed to look. It wouldn't surprise me if it would affect my decision-making. Who

doesn't want to get the pat on the back from the manager instead of the negative feedback?

Riley is not alone in her perception of following the rules. In fact, 15% of participants admitted to not calling a team because of the impact it had on their weekly efficiency reports. Millie disclosed,

> I often see interpreters not calling a team because that's another stat that you are monitored—um, how many times you call a team, for a percentage. So I've heard and also myself I've felt like "oh I can't call a team because I've already called a team before like twice today." You know? So I think that is unfortunate. But the company does, you know, does say if you need a team definitely call a team.

Although several participants expressed that their provider's tracking of instances of teaming influenced their decision to call for a team, several other participants reported that regardless of the impact it had on their numbers, they used their professional judgment and called for a team any time they deemed it necessary. For example, Jill reported that she called for a team any time she felt it was necessary and, if asked by management, she could justify each time that she requested a team. Similarly, Holly said, "To be tracked on how often you call for a team I think is um, I think is a little obtuse, and goes against what we as a field have fought to achieve—to make sure that we have that support there." Holly argued that she would call for a team if needed, but she was conscious of how teaming would impact her stats and her ability to obtain future work. Heidi, who had recently opted to reduce her weekly hours due to a concern she had regarding her manager's business/monetary perspective of interpreting, had been called to her manager's office for calling a team too frequently. Heidi confidently stated,

> My teaming average is closer to 10% when the average is supposed to be about 3%. My manager called me in and said, "You call teams too much, I don't understand. Do we need to retrain you on something? I think you're a really good interpreter." Like, "I don't understand why you're doing this." I'm like, "Do you not think that 10% of these calls would need a team? In community work would you have a team? If it was legal or really medical? We have zero context."

Heidi expressed that she could make a case to support every instance in which she called for a team. She was not concerned that she would get written up because she could defend her decisions for each incident; however, her provider's expectations of her efficiency did not align with her goal of providing quality service. Her efficiency report, which is evaluated quantitatively and represents her success as an employee, suggested that she may need additional training.

The notion of teaming is often associated with the length of an interaction and/or the complexity of the call. In Heidi's case, her manager assumed that she needed additional training so that she could reduce her need for a team in the future. In fact, participants noted requesting a team for different reasons, such as the emotional nature of the call. During the course of a VRS shift, it is impossible to predict with full certainty the topic of each call. Although some calls are more routine, and therefore predictable, than others (e.g., ordering pizza, making a doctor's appointment, calling a child's school), an unanticipated call can happen at any time. A call may be considered emotional in nature for a number of reasons. It may contain emotional content for the callers themselves, but the content may also strike a chord with the CA as well. For example, Dr. S expressed,

> I called for a team one time because it was such an emotional call and it involved a child. My team got there and I kind of brought up Word Pad on my computer so that I could secretly type, in real big letters, so they could see what's going on, cause the white board is too hard to write on. Um, so when my team got there um they were like looking at the screen and ready you know to delve in and I typed on the screen I said "Emotional call, I just need you beside me." And so she put her hand on my knee the whole time and then she was just there.

The action of calling a team for emotional support was raised by several participants. It was often referenced in discussions pertaining to stress, burnout, and call content that was perceived as high stakes (e.g., medical, legal) or sensitive in nature (e.g., death in family, situations involving children). Similarly to Dr. S's experience, Jill shared a story in which she perceived that she was not the appropriate person to interpret a call. In this situation, she elected to switch roles with the monitor interpreter; however, she remained with the team to provide the background knowledge that she had acquired from the beginning of the call. Dr. S and Jill both demonstrated professional autonomy by using reason and ethics to guide their decisions, regardless of whether they perceived that they had the freedom to act in this manner.

Jill's actions showed her ability to identify calls as particularly sensitive for personal reasons and consider appropriate solutions. Interviews with other CAs showed similar instances in which CAs recognized their biases and/or reactivity and removed themselves from a call altogether. Rose, who had worked as a CA for 7 years, noted a time that she teamed with a colleague who had a strong personal response to a particular call's content. She said,

> [The interpreter] had a call about abortion and her beliefs didn't coincide with how the call was going, so she was like "you need to take this call" because she was like stiff as a board and couldn't move. She was so flustered by the content of the call.

VRS provider software typically contains a mechanism that allows CAs to transfer a call to a new CA located at a different call center. Rose expressed that she was aware that her provider frowned upon transferring a call to a different call center (as opposed to calling for a team within the call center). In addition, she expressed that by transferring the call, "the other interpreter may go, 'Oh, it's a hand-off,' which has a negative connotation to it already. We only dump calls in hand-offs. That's what people think." Rose uses the term "hand-off" in reference to the act of transferring a call to another call center. Similar to a hand-off in football, in which the ball is handed to a nearby teammate to continue with the play, the act of handing off a VRS call indicates the action of passing the call to another CA to take the lead role from that point forward. In this instance, the CA used her professional judgment and determined that it was necessary she remove herself from the call given her personal bias regarding the topic of abortion. Rose provided an example of a similar experience in which she personally felt she could not continue with a call. She said,

> My late husband died of suicide and I found him. He died 3 months before I started working with VRS. Well you know the funny thing about VRS, you never know what's going to come at you and sometimes that type of situation comes at me. And I had a really hard time dealing with that. Um, so you're not allowed to switch it, heck if I'm not allowed. I can't deal with it. I'm switching it. And I'm happy to explain myself if somebody wants to know why.

Rose had several options in this situation. She could have called for a team to support her (as the provider expected); she could have called for a team and then removed herself from the call, leaving the new CA in her place (which also would have been an acceptable act according to the provider's expectations); or she could have transferred the call. Rose decided to switch the call to a different CA outside of her call center. She described her decision-making process:

> If the caller says that they want another interpreter, we can switch them. If they need a male interpreter, we can switch them. If they need Spanish, we can switch them. So there are so many other avenues of reasons to switch a client out that I don't really have to explain myself. I feel that I owe that to my clients to step out when it's not appropriate.

Given the multitude of other reasons that would justify transferring a call, she did not think that this singular instance would be brought to her attention in the form of disciplinary action. Rose noted that deaf people have the right to request a different CA for varying reasons. She was correct in her assessment, as stated in the Telecommunications Relay Service Rules (2011), "The TRS provider must make their best effort to accommodate the caller's preferred CA gender." Of course, it is similarly expected that Rose would transfer a call if it required interpretation between American Sign Language (ASL) and Spanish. Rose views her own needs as a human being as no different than those of callers.

Rose's ability to self-monitor her reaction and determine she was not the appropriate person to interpret for a sensitive topic is an example of self-care. With these decisions, Rose was applying energy to not only the interpreting process, but also to the self-analysis process. After reflecting about her ability to interpret on this topic, Rose removed herself from the situation. Rose noted that she expressed care for the caller by recognizing her emotional response and switching to another CA before she might impact the call. She also elected to switch with a CA who worked in her center (as opposed to transferring to another call center) out of concern that the call would get disconnected during the transfer process. By addressing the needs of the interpretation as well as managing her own emotions, Rose demonstrated care for the consumer and herself.

The following four actions were identified by participants as the primary ways in which CAs exercise professional autonomy in the face of management's tracking of CA work: (a) purposeful scheduling, (b) taking action in response to abusive callers, (c) modeling realistic expectations of performance, and (d) teaming. Additional acts of professional autonomy were also discussed by the participants throughout the interviews.

For example, CAs expressed that they often asked deaf callers for physical changes (e.g., lighting, camera positioning) to reduce the effects of eye strain in their work. Professional decisions can even be seen to take place prior to beginning to work in the VRS industry. Joy, who had worked for VRS for 9 months, said that she had considered working in VRS for a while but had concerns about the work. She had heard from colleagues that the provider in her area focused heavily on productivity and that CAs were evaluated based on statistical reports. Joy was not comfortable working within this type of system. Finally, when Joy heard that a smaller provider was coming to town that was not as focused on numbers, she immediately signed up. When recalling her experience, Joy said,

> I felt like I needed—this is gonna sound very needy and I'm not a needy person—but I felt like I needed more emotional support to be able to thrive in VRS because VRS was not something that I set out to do when I became an interpreter.

Joy was in the middle of a move to a new state and wanted to consider VRS as a potential source of income as she was getting settled. She reported that she was very fortunate to have the opportunity to work in VRS anywhere that she moved, but she wanted to be sure that she worked in a supportive environment. This can be considered a professional decision made prior to beginning work in VRS.

Chapter 4

Providing Customer Service

Although customer service is often viewed from a business standpoint, it should also be examined as a social interaction (Bolton & Houlihan, 2005). As customers, we interact with service providers on a daily basis both in person (e.g., servers in restaurants) and from a distance via telephone communication (e.g., bank tellers, store representatives). Bolton and Houlihan (2005) investigated interactions between customers and those who work in a call center environment. They describe the stance of customers in three different ways. In their interactions with call center representatives, customers may be viewed as *mythical sovereigns* who want a service as quickly as possible, *functional transactants* who want to carry out a transaction simply and efficiently, or *moral agents* who engage in communication and recognize the interaction as socially relevant (Bolton & Houlihan, 2005). Bolton and Houlihan argue that people cannot be categorized because their stance may change depending on the particular situation.

Similar to customers, employees who work in a call center are actors in these social interactions. Rafaeli, Ziklik, and Doucet (2008) identified the following five customer orientation behaviors used by employees in a bank call center: (a) anticipating customer requests (i.e., offering information prior to the customer explicitly asking for it), (b) offering explanations or justifications (i.e., explaining the procedure that will take place to fulfill the customer's needs), (c) educating the customer (i.e., teaching the customer company terminology or procedure so that the customer can handle future calls), (d) providing emotional support (i.e., giving positive or supportive emotional statements used to build rapport or show empathy), and (e) offering personalized information (i.e., providing customer-specific information to the caller). The presence of these customer orientation behaviors led to customer perception of better service quality. Throughout the study on CAs, it was repeatedly stated by CAs that their decisions were influenced by a desire to provide quality customer service to callers, and indeed, they exhibited some of the customer orientation behaviors identified by Rafaeli et al. (2008). In this chapter, I highlight ways in which the decisions made by CAs were influenced by the goal of providing quality customer service; I also highlight the ways that their actions aligned with the list of customer orientation behaviors identified by Rafaeli et al.

All of the participants reported that their desire to provide quality customer service influenced their decisions as a CA. In response to their desire to provide good customer service, the following six actions were taken by participants in this study: (a) choosing a specific team (30%), (b) staying late or skipping a scheduled break (35%), (c) cultural mediation (75%), (d) sharing visual information for emergency calls (55%), (e) switching to a different interpreter (40%), and (f) troubleshooting problems with technology and trying to reconnect (30%).

CHOOSING A SPECIFIC TEAM

As described earlier, CAs in VRS may evaluate a VRS call and determine that a second CA (i.e., a team) is necessary. In these situations, two CAs collaborate in an effort to ensure the accuracy of the message. While the act of teaming may appear similar from one provider to another, the provider-established rules associated with teaming and the method of requesting a team may differ.

Participants in this study had worked for varying VRS providers, each using different software to handle call routing and team requests. A common theme shared among participants, regardless of the provider, was that the software developed by the provider automatically selected the next available CA. By selecting the next available CA (as opposed to the most qualified), a team will arrive to the needed station as quickly as possible to offer support for the call; however, the supporting team member may not have the appropriate skills to interpret the call. Participants reported selecting and/or rejecting teams based on their judgment about the needs of each call. The topic of selecting a specific team member during a call was raised by 30% of the participants. The action of requesting or rejecting a specific team was described as being based on the CA's goal of providing quality customer service and ensuring the accuracy of the interpretation.

Bella, who worked 15 hours per week in VRS and had experience working for two different providers, explained that she used the call center's software chat feature to screen teams. The software is often used for communication among employees both within and across call centers. When used, the software displays a list of the CAs who are working at any given time. Bella said,

> I will admittedly look at the list and see who's there that day and be like, "What are the percent chances that I'm gonna get a person who can do X?" And every once in a while now, I would call a hearing team and if they weren't providing support be like "Can you see if the Deaf interpreter is available?"

Bella was fortunate to have the option of working with a deaf interpreter (DI) at her call center. DIs are native users of American Sign Language (ASL) who can draw from their life experiences as Deaf people in order to provide a culturally and linguistically appropriate interpretation (Forestal, 2011). DIs work alongside other interpreters in a multitude of settings (e.g., conference, mental health) in order to provide access for deaf individuals. Not all VRS providers offer DI services. In addition, even if a provider offers DI services, the DI may not be available due to other responsibilities, including actively supporting another CA with another call.

Like Bella, Riley could request a team by clicking a button on her computer screen. When a team was available, a message would pop up on her screen identifying the CA who would serve as her team. Riley admitted to clicking another button to cancel the request when she recognized that the available CA was not an appropriate match for the needs of the call. She shared,

> There are times when I would call for a team and see who the team is that's coming and I would cancel the request. I would cancel the request, give it a second and put out another request and get a different interpreter. And then I'd just have to be like, you know, I'd hate to say it, but little white lie if the person got there, "oh I don't need it anymore."

Bella and Riley weighed the decision of whether to work with the assigned CA (who they perceived as not an appropriate fit for the call) or cancel the request and start the process of requesting a team all over again. Assessing the strength of the team as a whole is an example of using professional reason and ethics to improve customer service; however, the system in which VRS takes place does not always support this action. Teams are assigned based on availability as opposed to skill. Regardless of the automated technology used to govern teaming in VRS, both CAs exercised professional autonomy in their decision making.

Levi recounted a specific call for which he determined that a particular person would be the best team:

> [I had a caller who was] a very avid sewer, and not a homebody, but they make their own clothes. And I said, "You know, I'm sorry, hold on one minute," and I grabbed [another interpreter] and I pulled her in like, "I have no idea what [she's] saying" and you know I'm getting red-faced like that and the customer's looking at me and laughing and she understands, like, honestly I have no idea what [she's] saying. Like I understand what [she's] saying, but I have no idea how to like—with classifiers—[express] what [she's] talking about.

Emily, like Levi, also noted that the topic of the call might lead her to request a specific team. Like Bella, Emily often used her call center's chat feature for support. She explained that her first step after determining that she needed support was to place a general request for a team. Then she would skim the list of available CAs on her computer, identify a team she felt would be an appropriate support for the call, and send that person a chat message to join her when available. She said,

> You never know if the [team that you want] is on a call and how long their call is gonna last, so it's better just to be safe and get somebody there. And maybe say "once you're off the call" if I know this specific person is real good with car mechanics or technology or whatever, get a team now and then [send a message] "when you are free please come over and switch out" or whatever.

Emily was 56 years old at the time of our meeting and had worked typically 15 hours a week as a CA for the past 5 years. She stated that she had become aware of her colleagues' specialized skills and preferred to work with someone who had the knowledge needed to ensure the call's success. She reported that she would take this action if the call was legal in nature since she did not hold the specialized legal certification offered by the Registry of Interpreters for the Deaf (RID) and was unfamiliar with legal terminology. She said, "I think three of us in our center have legal certification. So now that I know that, if it's a legal call I would definitely ask for one of those specific people." She also expressed that her decision to request a specific team for a call that presented with legal terminology was based on her desire to provide an accurate interpretation and quality customer service. Similarly to Bella, Riley, and Levi, Emily exercised professional autonomy regardless of the automated technology used to govern teaming in VRS.

CAs reported staying late (after their shift has ended) or skipping scheduled breaks in an effort to offer quality customer service. These actions are identifiable in provider reports of CA work and contrast with decisions influenced by corporate tracking of CA productivity. VRS providers have varied policies regarding staying after a shift has ended. As stated earlier, VRS providers screen CAs prior to hiring, and those hired are considered generalists who can interpret any call with a certain degree of efficacy. With the view that CAs are interchangeable, VRS providers may hold the expectation that one CA can start a call and another can step in to finish the call if the first CA leaves. Of course, providers often recommend that the CA call for a team to observe the call with enough time to become familiar with the call content before switching out. The topic of preferring to stay late or skipping a scheduled break in order to finish a call in its entirety was raised by 35% of CA participants.

Red discussed several reasons for staying late or skipping a break, including the perceived importance of the call, the ability to establish trust or rapport with the caller, and the consequences of switching CAs if the caller preferred not to share that there is a CA on the line. Red's reasons for his decision to stay late are driven by the same overarching goal: providing quality customer service. He expressed that he always made a judgment call, "Would transferring [the call] negatively impact the caller worse than it would negatively impact me that I have to stay here? And if the answer is yes, I would always be willing to stay." Red shared that he was willing to transfer a call if he knew that there was enough time for the next interpreter to build rapport with the caller; however, he said that for varying reasons he was willing to stay late, even past the call center's scheduled closing time if needed. He shared,

> I mean break is nothing, end of shift, closing of the center. You've gotta really make that call. I've stayed late many times I would say. This call is too important. Or a lot of times I've even done it when they say, "Don't tell them it's VRS because they really have a hard time." Well now I can't transfer you because it's gonna become obvious. I'm not gonna reveal it's VRS by switching so I'll stay on for longer with a consistent voice.

Red's response appears in some ways paternalistic, as his caretaking could be considered a way of managing the deaf caller; however, his actions show the use of personal decision making based on his call analysis. Similarly, Louise noted that, for the sake of ensuring customer service, she considered the amount of background knowledge (e.g., names, events, goal of caller) that had already been shared with the CA. She recounted an experience in which a deaf person had previously shared her personal information (e.g., credit card number, Social Security number) during a phone scam. In this situation, a hearing caller had falsely represented his identity in order to obtain the deaf caller's personal information. After realizing that she had been victim to a scam, the deaf caller reached out to her bank to file a claim. With the goal of supporting this caller, Louise stayed late after her shift had ended. She said, "All that background knowledge would have been hard to pass on to another interpreter and it would have made [the caller] have to start all over again, and it would have been such a longer process." Louise already knew the story of what had happened, the date that it had occurred, and the amount of money lost. She felt that transferring the call to another CA would have been an additional burden on the deaf caller, who had already been through an emotional ordeal. Louise exercised autonomy in response to the power imbalance that existed between the deaf caller who fell victim to a scam and the bank that could potentially help the deaf caller protect her money.

Joy, who worked in VRS 25 to 30 hours per week, also referenced the amount of background knowledge that she accumulated during a call and how leaving before the call ended would be a disservice to the deaf customer. She shared,

> I have stayed late several times and it is not usually like 5 or 10 minutes late, it's almost always 45 minutes to an hour later. Just the nature of the type of call, the harder that they are to pass off the more involved they are, which means they take longer. I feel like to start that over with somebody else would really interrupt the flow of the conversation. I just think if the purpose is for us to serve our customers in the best way possible, the best way possible is just smooth communication. So they can have an uninterrupted conversation.

In an effort to ensure that calls were seamless and customers were satisfied with their communication experience, the CAs in this study exercised their professional autonomy by staying after their shifts had ended. They were not comfortable leaving in the middle of a call if they perceived that their leaving would negatively impact the quality of the caller's experience. This behavior is similar to how time is managed in community work (e.g., medical, education). Whether or not providers responded favorably to the action of staying late or skipping a break was not discussed during the interviews.

CULTURAL MEDIATION

Gustafsson, Norström, and Fieretos (2013) define culture as "those parts of human interaction that are collective and which concern everyday life, the creation of meaning, values, customs and habits" (p. 189). Furthermore, cultural brokering or mediating is the use of cultural competence in order to "bridge cultural differences in multicultural contexts" (Gustafsson et al., 2013, p. 190). Interpreters are present in instances of discourse among people whose language, background, and culture differ from those of others. In such interactions, the interpreter is often the only person present who understands both parties; therefore, interpreters serve as cultural mediators regulating communication. Pöchhacker (2004) stated that interpreters serve as "an intermediary, not so much between the languages involved as between the communicating individuals and the institutional and socio-cultural positions they represent" (p. 59). Pöchhacker offered the example of turn-taking to demonstrate how an interpreter may regulate the flow of communication. The interpreter's role is that of a mediator, whose goal is to ensure understanding among conversational participants.

As previously mentioned, VRS is still in its infancy; therefore, depending on the frequency with which both deaf and hearing individuals use the service, callers may be unfamiliar with conditions that are common in the telecommunication environment (e.g., phone trees, scam calls, "do not announce"). The findings of this study on CAs indicate that CAs' decision making during each call is influenced by their desire to culturally mediate in situations in which either the hearing or the deaf conversational participant is not accustomed to VRS. Instances of cultural mediation are reflections of Rafaeli et al.'s (2008) customer orientation behaviors. For example, exercising professional autonomy, a CA may educate a deaf caller about robo calls, scams, navigating phone trees, or any other new information that they may not be aware of prior to this instance. Educating customers is the third customer orientation behavior observed in Rafaeli et al.'s study. Similarly, a CA may use professional autonomy by offering explanations of a particular procedure (i.e., the second customer orientation behavior). An example of this may occur when the deaf person shares a phone number with a hearing caller who audibly seems confused as to how he could possibly call the deaf person using the phone. In this instance, the CA may use their professional autonomy to mediate the interaction by explaining to the hearing caller that calling the deaf person would result in connecting the hearing caller to a CA and the call would proceed as in the present call, although with a different CA.

Within the theme of cultural mediation, the most frequent topic addressed by participants was dealing with phone trees. Phone trees are automated telephone systems often used by businesses and organizations to direct calls to particular units (e.g., billing, technical support) through the use of fixed menus of call routing options. The caller can select an option from the menu by pressing a particular phone key, speaking keywords, or repeating short phrases. Phone trees are designed to route calls based on programmed responses. During interviews, 60% of participants expressed that their actions were influenced by their desire to assist callers with the navigation of a phone tree. Decisions during VRS calls were made that demonstrated the following actions: (a) offering to push zero; (b) telling the caller the actions they are taking (i.e., the number they selected) to get to the right person; and (c) asking for further information regarding the topic in question in order to determine the correct menu selection.

Holly explained that to ensure the success of calls, she not only offered to push zero, but also educated the caller that if zero is pushed, the call will likely be transferred to a live customer representative. She said,

> You know, some deaf people get [phone trees] and some deaf people just don't get it, which is fine, it's such a hearing thing. And so [in this situation] I kinda stepped over my boundaries and I said, "Do you wanna talk to a live person?" and they were like, "Yes that's what I want." I was like, "Okay, I'm gonna go ahead and push zero." There's no option to do that, but I know as a hearing person that if I hit zero we're gonna connect with somebody and this person's gonna get what they want.

Holly recognized that she was adding the option of pushing zero to reach a representative, which was not originally offered by the automated phone tree system. However, she opined that this was not an ethical violation; rather, it was an act of customer service. As deaf callers become more familiar with phone trees, they may begin to predict their use when calling businesses or organizations. If so, the deaf caller may immediately request to speak with a "live person" (representative). By instructing the CA to listen to the options and independently choose the one that will most expeditiously route the call to a representative, the deaf caller is relinquishing power (such as call ownership) to the CA.

Instead of pushing zero, Cailin used the strategy of asking the caller for further information regarding the topic needing to be addressed. She said, "I might say 'Well, live person related to what?'" She knows that pushing zero may allow her to reach a representative; however, phone trees are often programmed to ask for additional information in an effort to lead the caller to the right representative in the correct department. To support this process, she often asked the caller for additional information in order to select the right prompt from the phone tree. Similarly, Sandy, who had worked as a CA for 3.5 years, agreed that there was an educational aspect to phone trees.

> If they don't know that you have to get through all of those options in a phone tree to get to this specific department, or to even just get to general service person or something, then how are they ever going to know that in the future if that's not communicated to them in some way? And I don't think it's my job to be educating people but I think it's a subtle form of education and just kind of information sharing. And again, it's just something that hearing people are used to. I think that just providing that visual access to that information even if it's not wanted (laughs), it's part of my job.

Sandy noted that deaf callers were often emphatically uninterested in learning about phone tree navigation. After appearing on screen, these callers immediately signed "LIVE PERSON," "REPRESENTATIVE," or "OPERATOR." These callers clearly expected the CA to take care of the rest and only inform them once connected to a person who would discuss their needs. Columbine reported that she often commiserated with the caller's frustration with phone trees in an effort to build rapport. Commiserating with the caller is an example of the fourth customer orientation behavior (i.e., providing emotional support) listed by Rafaeli et al. (2008). Columbine explained that she often said to the caller,

> "We will get a live person but you have to pick which live person." You know, "Do you need the accounting person? Do you need billing?

What do you need?" I always interpret the options, no matter if they say, "I want a live person." "All right, we will get there, but first which of these do you want? Push zero? O.K. I'll push zero and we'll see what happens." And I will let the deaf person know "I hate these systems too, but we gotta get through this."

Phone trees are not the only situation in which CAs conducted cultural mediation. The participants also reported that they perceived members of the deaf community as being unfamiliar with calls from people attempting to defraud them (i.e., scam calls).

There are often auditory cues associated with a call that is a scam (e.g., hearing caller has strong foreign accent, presence of strange background noise) as well as visual cues (e.g., phone number is not available, phone number is not associated with the location that the caller claims to be from). CAs often expressed that it is not their place to assume that a call is a scam and blatantly tell the deaf person that the person they are speaking with is lying; however, as native English speakers, CAs are able to read between the lines and identify these types of calls. The perception that the deaf community is unable to identify dishonest callers may lead CAs to act in response. These actions can potentially be described as advocacy; however, the CA participants often referred to these actions as customer service. If the CA perceived the call was most likely a scam, the CA often used strategies to hint to the deaf caller that there was something strange about the call. Heidi shared,

> I've seen a lot of interpreters tell them "No, it's a scam" or whatever. I don't believe that I can ethically do that. It's incredibly hard to watch someone give away their credit card number and Social Security number, and whatever else. I will say like, "Strong accent, hard to understand, seems international" or "the connection is bad." Um, I will ask for repetition more often unless I clearly understand what they said, but that's my own I guess linguistic way of trying to show that it is a scam.

Heidi drew on her sense of personal ethics to suggest that the caller may be untrustworthy. However, her strategy to cue the deaf caller to the possibility that the hearing person on a call is untrustworthy is not unique. Sharon, a CA for 9.5 years, debriefed with a colleague after she experienced a call that she perceived as a scam.

> That was a serious ethical dilemma, you know? In general interpreters think they just have to interpret because of the FCC. But it's like, "Okay,

but our ethics say do no harm and we know this is a scam. So what can we do about this?" So, a Spanish interpreter said to me once, because I got off a call and I just went, "This is horrible. Calling on the day they get their [Social Security] check." And so she said, "Why don't you make a face when they start asking for money?" I'm like O.K., so the next time [I got] a call "You will win one thousand dollars—one million dollars if you . . ." so I made this crazy face, and it worked. The deaf person said, "Is this a scam?"

Sharon noted that the RID Code of Professional Conduct (CPC) states that the interpreter is to "do no harm"; however, the notion of harm pertains to acts committed by the interpreter, not those carried out by either the deaf or hearing callers. The CPC does not recommend that the interpreter alert deaf people of perceived misrepresentations or inaccuracies expressed by hearing people. Participants agreed that it was not their place to advise callers what to do with their money or how to care for their personal information; however, they expressed that they wanted to at least try to alert the caller of a perceived potential scam. The decisions CAs made in these situations suggest a strong alignment with deaf callers. It is of note that no participants raised the topic of supporting their hearing callers in a similar manner.

Cultural mediation did not just occur in situations in which deaf people had minimal experience with current telecommunication culture; CAs also mediated instances in which hearing people were unfamiliar with VRS and/or were not aware that a CA was on the line. Commonly, these calls begin with the deaf person saying to the CA, "NOT ANNOUNCE," which is a signal from the deaf caller to the CA that the call should not begin with an opening script that informs the hearing caller that the call will take place through an interpreter. By identifying that there is a third party (i.e., the CA) on the line, hearing callers who are familiar with VRS (e.g., family member, colleague) know that there may be some short periods of silence during the interpreting process or that they may need to more clearly explain information that may be unfamiliar to the CA (e.g., spelling of names). In other instances, when the hearing caller is unfamiliar with VRS, introducing the call by announcing that there is an interpreter on the line may be confusing for the hearing person or cause apprehension regarding the call.

The deaf person may decide to tell the CA not to announce that the call is taking place through an interpreter for a number of reasons. The decision may simply stem from personal preference or concern that the call will not be accepted because of the presence of the interpreter as a third party. Representatives at financial institutions often tell deaf customers that they cannot accept the call directly and that the call should be made using the designated "hearing impaired" phone number, usually a teletypewriter (TTY)-dedicated line. However, deaf callers may not have access to a TTY or may prefer to use a videophone. Regardless of the reason, CAs frequently interpret for situations in which the hearing caller is not aware that there is a third party on the line. To maintain discretion, the CA may decide to use a number of strategies.

The following two strategies were described by CA participants for managing calls in which they were directed to not announce their presence: (a) inserting fillers such as sharing visual information that was not explicitly stated by the deaf caller but could be seen by the CA via video (25%), and (b) decreasing their processing time (i.e., the time between the expression of the source message and the conveying of the target message) so as not to allow for long periods of silence (15%). One participant, Tux, acknowledged that hearing people are often uncomfortable with lengthy periods of silence over the phone; she shared that with long periods of silence, often "the hearing person is going 'Hello? Are you O.K.? Are you there?' [So I use fillers such as] 'Yeah give me a second, I'm looking at the paper so hold on.'" To alleviate any awkwardness, Red said,

> With the "do not announce" you have to do a lot to maintain the flow and still portray [the deaf person's] goal of making it seamlessly not a VRS call. So a lot more of the fillers like "actually yeah and the reason I was calling was . . . umm . . . if you wouldn't mind just wait one second I'm trying to . . ."

Aside from fillers, CAs reported that they often reduced the amount of time between the deaf caller's question or comment (i.e., the source language utterance) and the conveying of the interpretation in English (i.e., the target language utterance) with the goal of minimizing long periods of silence. Riley shared, "I try to be as close [in time to the message delivered by the deaf person] as possible because when they start hearing big delays, you constantly get the 'Hello? Hello?' and MESS-UP [the flow of the call is disrupted]." Another strategy expressed by participants was offering to transfer to an interpreter of the same gender as the deaf caller in order to minimize confusion that might arise from the voice not matching the expectations of the hearing conversational participant.

During a VRS call, CAs have visual access to deaf callers and their surrounding environment (e.g., home, office). As a result of this visual access, CAs may feel as though they are "present" in what they perceive to be an emergency. Of the 20 participants in the CA study, 11 (55%) raised the topic of feeling responsible for sharing visual information to ensure the safety and well-being of their deaf consumers.

The decision to share information that was not explicitly stated by the deaf caller may be influenced by a number of factors. The most obvious trigger that spurred CAs to include visual information was if the call presented as a 911 call. These calls often have a unique ring tone that identifies them as emergency calls; however, participants reported sharing visible information from the call-in situations that they perceived as emergencies, regardless of whether the call was, in fact, being made to a 911 call center.

During the interview session, Bella recollected a VRS call in which a female caller was a survivor of domestic violence and was trying to get to a shelter. She explained,

> [The caller] kept saying "He's gonna be here, he's gonna be here" and he [was], he showed up and he shut the call down. [In that situation] I explained a lot more of what I saw, visually, to the caller, to the hearing person, and I tried to reconnect. And that's okay, if we disconnect from that person we can call, we can try to reconnect so I tried and tried and tried but it was blocked.

Bella exercised professional autonomy in hopes that the visual information would be enough to support the hearing caller in their effort to help this woman. Rose provided an example of an instance in which she shared information that was visibly present in the call. The call was directed to 911 after a car accident. Rose said,

> In the car accident situation [I told the 911 operator] "I see two people. I can't understand what they're saying. The picture is blurred out. One's injured. They need an ambulance. I can see blood." Then I could see them [so I added], "Oh, the other person is really dizzy. They're nauseous. They just vomited. It looks light outside. There's a building, a red brick building in the background."

Rose explained that the goal was to get emergency services to the right location in order to help these people. Because the call originated from a cell phone, the location of the caller could not be identified. Rose used her professional autonomy and determined that by sharing visible information she could help emergency services identify the location of the car accident.

Another participant, Jill, experienced a similar call in which the goal was to get emergency services to an unidentified location. She shared,

> If I don't know where they are because they're calling on mobile, that's gonna change the way that I approach the situation. It's going to be the first thing that we take care of. I'm already starting to look for things that can help dispatch locate this person.

Data in this study suggest that CAs frequently include information that they determine is necessary in order to ensure the safety and well-being of the caller. This can include both visual and auditory information. For example, Joy worked for a provider that used software that allowed the CA to have auditory access to the deaf caller's surroundings. She used both visual and auditory information during a call to 911 for a woman who reported an intruder in her home. Joy shared,

> Instead of just interpreting the words that are being said, you know, I give extra information. Things like "I'm having trouble seeing the caller because it appears they are locked in a closet." You know, "They've put themselves in a closet" rather "I'm not able to see them clearly enough [to interpret]." You know, other things like "Yes it sounds like the other person is still in the room." Situational stuff, like, "This is what I can see and what I can hear," as opposed to just the language.

Participants expressed that providers do not have official rules against providing visual information and trying to reconnect emergency calls. In fact, some providers encourage CAs to share visual information during 911 calls. Interviews showed that CAs do not necessarily simply follow the rules established by their providers, but rather also use their professional autonomy to conduct a personal assessment of the needs of each call and to respond in the way they feel is most appropriate. For example, Heidi, who worked approximately 20 hours per week as a CA, received a call in which the caller asked her for personal advice.

> [The caller] starts crying and she's like "What would you do if your stepfather raped you?" and I asked her "Call 911?" All I needed was a yes. Any movement, anything to indicate yes, but my thought was if I

call 911, they're gonna send someone to the house, which, if she won't say anything, is gonna make things worse for her. She just stared at me and then she hung up.

Although this caller did not make the call to 911 and no visual information was shared, Heidi used her professional autonomy in what she deemed to be an emergency situation. She decided not to contact emergency services and not to reconnect the call. Heidi's decision is in contrast with the example in which Bella continued to try to reconnect to the caller who had experienced domestic violence. Clearly, CAs are using their ethical decision-making to gauge the effect that their actions might have on the callers. The decision to use visual information in an interpretation to support the well-being of the caller is one such action.

SWITCHING TO A DIFFERENT INTERPRETER

During interviews, CAs often expressed that the providers for whom they work had formal policies stating that CAs ought to accept all calls and potentially seek the support of a team if needed. Regardless of these overt provider guidelines, 50% of the participants raised the topic of personally determining whether they are the appropriate CA for the call. The goal of providing quality customer service was the driving force behind their decisions to offer the services of a different CA and remove themselves from the call. CAs commonly expressed the understanding that they were not a match for every call. They shared that in some cases this determination stemmed from the perceived frustration of the caller in response to the interpretation; whereas in other cases, they perceived their own personal response to the content of the call and decided to switch to a different CA.

Tux explained that she was aware of the Federal Communications Commission (FCC) policy that CAs accept all calls; however, if she recognized that either the interpretation was not accurate or the client was not happy, she would offer the caller the opportunity to work with a different CA. She recalled a specific situation:

> Honestly, my solution [for this call] was to say, "I don't think we are a match. Do you mind if I transfer you to another interpreter?" and that was it. [They said] "O.K." I told the client, "I want to see you happy, I want you to be satisfied" and the person said "O.K."

Many CAs did not independently decide to transfer a call in which the deaf caller seemed dissatisfied but, rather, offered the deaf caller the opportunity to work with another person. In some situations, the caller preferred to continue with the current CA irrespective of complaints regarding the service. For example, Joy recalled, "I was told that I was a lousy interpreter. And I offered to let another interpreter proceed with the call and I was told 'Oh, no.'" In compliance with the deaf caller's wishes, Joy then continued with the call until its completion. Similarly, Riley had calls where the deaf caller seemed to become frustrated with the interpretation:

> If they start going INTERPRETER NOT UNDERSTAND or if they are having me voice, "The interpreter doesn't understand me"—I've done that, where I've said that for the hearing person and the Deaf person simultaneously, "Would you like me to transfer you to another interpreter?"

The goal of providing quality customer service also prompted CAs to self-assess whether they were inappropriate for a call due to personal reasons. These calls were often emotional in nature. Consequently, the CA often switched with another CA internally (within their call center) as opposed to transferring the call to a different call center. For example, Millie recounted a call that she perceived as being particularly emotional; she decided to call for a replacement:

> I called a team and then once the team was there, I asked them, "O.K. are you ready to take over?" Sometimes I feel that I'm not the right person to take that call because um, again relating back to customer service, um because like that caller would be better with another interpreter.

In the same manner, Rose expressed,

> I do an internal switch especially if it's a sensitive thing. So one time I would say maybe three or four years ago I had a person who was actively suicidal talking to a parent, and the parent didn't know what to say. So of course my little mental health brain goes "oh you're saying everything wrong." I had already called a team. I had worked with this team before on a suicidal call and she goes "get out of here." We switched seats, I left, she called for another team. That really is the best way to handle that situation because sending it out to a different center, what if they get disconnected? When handing off a call out of center disconnections happen sometimes.

Rose identified that she could not continue with this interpretation without altering the communication. It could be argued that Rose's personal experience coincided with the goal of the parent, which was to offer emotional support to their child. With this perspective, Rose would be well suited to continue with this interaction. However, Rose evaluated the situation and felt that it was best that she remove herself from the call. She expressed that she would be unable to continue with the call without having an emotional response that would prevent her from faithfully interpreting the message.

TROUBLESHOOTING PROBLEMS WITH TECHNOLOGY AND TRYING TO RECONNECT

As previously mentioned, the development of VRS technology changed not only the environment in which communication takes place (i.e., communication at a distance through signed language) but also the dynamics of the interaction. In reaction to the technology, CAs often troubleshoot problems with VRS software as well as try to reconnect with callers who are experiencing technical difficulty. Often, VRS providers have specific departments dedicated to technical support and protocols directing callers to these support centers. If a CA is working with a deaf caller to resolve a technical difficulty, this is time that the CA is not connected to both a deaf and hearing caller and, therefore, not producing billable minutes. CAs exercise autonomy by supporting callers in their effort to resolve technical issues regardless of the provider's rules discouraging this behavior. In line with Rafaeli et al.'s (2008) fifth customer orientation behavior, troubleshooting VRS technology with a caller can be considered offering personalized information that does not pertain to the specific call in question but may be helpful to the caller. Discussions surrounding the actions taken when technical difficulty arises were initiated by 30% of the participants.

Given the amount of time that CAs spend working in VRS, they are often familiar with tricks that may help to resolve technical problems. Emily, who had worked as a CA for the past 5 years, shared,

Often times [the caller] can see us clearly but we can't see them, it's pixelated. So, you know, letting them know, "I can't see you, do you want me to hang up and call again?" 'cause sometimes that does clear up the picture. Not always, but once in a while. So they will make the decision. You know, "Do you want to hang up and I'll call again or do you want to try to call another interpreter?"

Rather than notifying the caller of technical difficulty, ending the call, and connecting to a new call, Emily exercises autonomy by offering a potential solution. Riley took a similar approach by trying to work with a deaf caller to resolve video quality.

I'll talk to the person that's having the tech issue to make sure there's nothing that they can do. Um, I'll make sure that they are aware of what I'm seeing because sometimes they'll know that somebody else in the house is using the internet at the same time so they can get that person off and get better video quality. Um, I will suggest possibly having them troubleshoot to the point that I can troubleshoot with them.

Riley exercised professional autonomy with the goal of providing good customer service. In fact, CAs often empathized with a caller's frustration and tried to resolve the issue by disconnecting and then reconnecting the call. Jill, who had been a CA for 3 years, recognized that experiencing technical difficulty may result in the deaf caller having to hang up and start the call over with a new CA. She shared,

I try to reconnect because that usually means that we have already established rapport or a relationship. And I just think that's tough on deaf people if it's like "I connect and now I gotta go to another interpreter and I gotta start all over again."

Attempting to reconnect the call is an example of CAs exercising professional autonomy. CAs are making decisions in support of deaf callers regardless of provider-initiated rules regarding the number of times a CA may try to reconnect. Louise, who had been a CA for 1 year, said that her provider set a limit on how long she could wait for a clear picture or how many times she could try to reconnect, after which she was expected to disconnect the call. She usually waited 30 seconds to see if the picture quality improved; however, if the problem did not resolve, she also empathized with how stressful it can be for a deaf person to experience technical difficulty. Louise considered the length of the call and the participants involved in the conversation when deciding how many times to try to reconnect. She shared,

If it's someone that has been on hold for 30 minutes and they are still on hold and they are going to lose their place in line, I'm going to try relatively hard to connect them back. If it's someone that just lost a connection because they are talking to their mom, and they can just call back in 5 minutes, I might try three times, three or four times and then disconnect.

During the process of troubleshooting technology, CAs also reported alerting the hearing caller of the problem. Columbine expressed that she often tried to alleviate any awkward silences by including the hearing caller in the discussion. During her interview, she said,

If the screen is really blurry, I try to include the hearing person as to what is going on at the same time, like "Thank you so much for your patience, this is just gonna be a little longer. Just give me one minute and we will see if we can get this issue fixed," making sure that both parties know what's going on.

CAs expressed empathy during the discussion of technical problems. Their decisions to act in response to problems associated with technology (i.e., cultural mediation) are evidence of their use of professional autonomy to provide quality customer service.

Throughout their interviews, CAs expressed limited professional autonomy in VRS and actively considered whether to use professional autonomy during VRS calls. The two major emerging themes identified as factors influencing the decision to use professional autonomy were as follows: (a) VRS provider tracking of CA work and the use of efficiency reports as a management tool, and (b) the goal of offering quality customer service to VRS callers. Given the link between CA decisions and the ability to obtain future work, it is little wonder that CAs express having limited autonomy. Regardless, CAs noted a variety of ways in which they expressed professional autonomy in response to the aforementioned themes.

Chapter 5

Lessons From the Past Inform the Future

Every day, deaf and hearing people around the world use video relay service (VRS) as a means to communicate with one another. Freedom of communication that was considered a dream not long ago has now become a reality through VRS. As this communication technology spreads, interpreting scholars have begun to examine various aspects of VRS labor, including its implications for interpreters and the deaf community (Bailey, 2005; Bower, 2013; Brunson, 2011; Brunson, 2018).

Interpreting in a setting that is dependent upon technology introduces challenges that are not present when interpreters are in the same location as communication participants. Skinner, Napier, and Braun (2018) note challenges such as lack of presence, knowledge of strategies in a remote interpreting environment, and interpreter authority. These complications may arise directly from the use of technology, such as is the case when there is a poor video connection due to internet limitations. In addition, the work of interpreters becomes increasingly complex due to the system in which VRS is offered. Brunson (2018) argues that "regardless of their employment classification, when they are working, interpreters are engaged and embedded in a bureaucracy" (p. 40). That bureaucracy carries with it rules and regulations to guide decision-making. Brunson goes on to say that it is important that we do not simply focus on the rules that constrain the work of interpreters, but rather shed light on the actions of interpreters within these environments. In this research study, I add to the investigation of VRS interpreting by examining how interpreters exercise professional autonomy in the video relay service setting despite constraints established by federal agencies and corporate entities. Twenty VRS interpreters throughout the United States were interviewed between November 2013 and November 2014 regarding their daily experience in VRS and the decisions they make in the VRS environment. Interview data were analyzed and revealed two primary themes regarding VRS interpreters' decision making. In addition, data indicated various actions interpreters take to express their professional autonomy, actions that sometimes run counter to established Federal Communications Commission (FCC) or provider-initiated rules.

Results suggest that the decisions made by VRS interpreters are constrained by the highly structured environment in which they work. Specifically, interpreters reported making decisions in an effort to bolster their efficiency reports, which are constantly tracked by their individual VRS employer. Participants reported that they often adhere to provider rules with the primary goal of obtaining their preferred schedules. By utilizing technology to track the actions of interpreters, and by rewarding interpreters with benefits such as shift selection, VRS providers may be encouraging interpreters to make decisions that support increased profit as opposed to quality of interpretation. In response to the tracking of their work by providers, interpreters may be making decisions that result in increased fatigue and, ultimately, burnout. As Brunson (2018) suggests, however, we cannot look solely at the influencing factors, but rather we must examine interpreters' decision making within the bureaucratic environment.

At the time of this study, the topic of provider constraints on VRS interpreting was prominent throughout the interviews; however, the most frequently discussed factor influencing decision making was providing quality customer service. Results suggest that CAs make professional decisions in their work based on the objective of providing high-quality service to their customers. For example, CAs reported staying late after their shift to close a call, asking for a specific team member for challenging calls, and doing additional work to troubleshoot problems with technology, among other actions. They were aware that such actions could negatively impact their efficiency report and thus their chances of obtaining the schedules they wished to work; however, they often reported that the goal of customer service took precedence over these other concerns.

This study's findings suggest a clear shift in the professional autonomy of signed language interpreters. Historically, interpreters were friends and family members of people within the deaf community who volunteered their services without formal organization or oversight. Without oversight, these early interpreters held complete autonomy over their work (Fant, 1990). The 1964 establishment of the Registry of Interpreters for the Deaf (RID) prompted the professionalization of the field of interpretation. The path of professionalization created structures such as certifications, a code of ethics, and educational programs (Wilensky, 1964); however, the field of ASL–English interpreting continues to evolve and reflects how interpreters view the role of deaf and hearing conversational participants, linguistic and cultural norms, and the interpreting community's own understanding of the power associated with their role. Over the past 50 years, philosophies have emerged depicting the role of interpreters in varying ways (Witter-Merithew, 1986). Interpreters' roles were not developed in isolation, but rather collectively, as interpreters, who were members of RID, were involved in the decision to portray their work in a specific manner.

Nearly four decades after RID's establishment, streamed video communication technology became available, resulting in a transformation in the practices of interpreters. Starting in April 2003, Sorenson Communications began distributing videophone technology to deaf people throughout the United States at no cost. The explosion of video technology instantaneously changed the way that interpreting services were provided to deaf people, including the organization and oversight of interpreting service provision. VRS is a federally funded for-profit industry with rules and regulations that constrain the autonomy of interpreters who work within the VRS environment. These constraints may be likened to the work of people who work in commercial call centers (e.g., technical support, product sales), an environment highly controlled by scripts and productivity measures. Brophy (2011) refers to call center work as highly automated "cognitive capitalism" (p. 410). The reports of interpreters working in VRS call centers (referred to as CAs) suggest a similar experience to other call center employees: CAs are connected to callers randomly through an automated system that shares minimal information about the callers. The CA is then tasked with providing effective customer service with little context on which to rely. The success of CAs is measured quantitatively using efficiency measures (e.g., speed of answer, percentage of time working with a team) as opposed to on the quality of their work. In light of the nature of VRS interpreting, Peterson (2011) argued that the work that occurs in the VRS environment does not qualify as interpreting at all, but rather as the "educated guessing" of call center employees (p. 203).

Rules established by individual VRS providers and FCC regulations prohibit the observation and recording of VRS calls, which protects caller confidentiality but also creates a barrier to research about VRS interpretation. However, the VRS research that is available supports Metzger's (1999) and Roy's (2000) claims that interpreters are active participants in these interactions. Studies suggest that CAs apply strategies in response to the demands of VRS (Bocian, 2012) and consciously make footing shifts in interpreted VRS interactions as needed (Marks, 2015). Taken together, these findings suggest that VRS is a structured language environment, in which interpreters are active communicative participants, despite the constraints that govern their work.

Control over the provision of interpreting services has moved into the realm of corporate decisions. Interpreters, who were originally the friends and family members of deaf people, are now educated at universities, screened by corporations, and evaluated quantitatively based on efficiency measures. Postman (1992) warned that new technologies often appear as solutions to the complexities of human life but may not fulfill that promise. The lure of technology is its predictability, efficiency, and standardization (Ritzer, 2008). Its success can be measured using quantitative methods. In these ways, technology can be "seductive" (Turkle, 2011, p. 1), offering deaf people access to telecommunication and offering interpreters a regular schedule, professional wages, and corporate benefits. However, corporations motivated by capitalist business practices control delivery of interpreting services in the VRS setting.

I heard someone once compare the automatization of VRS to a popular episode of *I Love Lucy* that first aired in September of 1952 (Oppenheimer, Davis, Carroll, & Asher, 1952). The television sitcom features Lucy, a plucky homemaker, and her husband Ricky in a variety of humorous domestic situations. In one particular episode, Lucy and her friend Ethel are challenged by their husbands to work outside the home for 1 week. Lucy and Ethel find employment at a chocolate factory, wrapping chocolates as the candies swiftly move down a conveyer belt. Their supervisor tells them that if they miss a single chocolate, they will be fired. With this threat in mind, as the conveyor belt increases speed, Lucy and Ethel begin to stuff chocolates into their mouths, hats, and down their shirts. When the manager returns to check on the pair, she is pleased that the chocolates are no longer on the belt and assumes that they have been successfully wrapped as required. Given the ease with which the pair seem to be working, the manager speeds up the conveyer belt in hopes of wrapping a greater number of chocolates.

The imagery evoked by the aforementioned episode of *I Love Lucy* can be applied to work in the VRS environment. Peterson (2011) writes, "we have reduced the professional authority of interpreters to that of assembly line workers" (p. 204). The interview data from this study do indeed suggest that interpreting in a VRS environment has elements of working on an assembly line, as in the sitcom. Advancements in communication technology have pushed the interpreting profession into a period of transition. Rather than leading the technology, however, interpreters (along with the deaf community) may have a sense of chasing it, trying to keep up. VRS providers develop rules and regulations that may be equally motivated by profit as by quality of service. This study indicates that interpreters continue to value quality service for the deaf community, which is evident in their frequent reference to customer service. At the same time, they report taking action outside of VRS calls, perceiving limited professional autonomy within the call. Although decisions that take place outside of calls, such as inserting breaks, are effective in alleviating individual concerns regarding the pace of work, CAs recognize these may be ineffective in evoking large-scale change to the system. Although Lucy might briefly step away from the conveyer belt, the speed of the oncoming chocolates does not abate. The decisions reported by VRS interpreters suggest a similar pattern.

Findings from this study indicate that the decisions CAs make are driven by the goal of providing customer service; however, they are also influenced by the corporate system under which they work. As the state of the interpreting field continues to evolve, the question of how interpreters respond to the technology and its corporate undertones remains. Do CAs in the VRS setting exercise their professional autonomy to make decisions regarding their work? Does the deaf community perceive VRS CAs as having the autonomy to act independently? Furthermore, do deaf people prefer speed of service over quality of interpretation? As our friend Lucy demonstrated, the conveyer belt may not be slowing down any time soon, and stuffing the chocolates into our hats does not make them disappear. Similarly, we must face the issues in VRS directly, with open minds and a readiness to shape the future.

Appendix A

A History of Telecommunications:

From Telegraph to Video Relay Service

Adapted from Lang (2000)

1837   Samuel F. B. Morse demonstrates the telegraph, the first electrically operated machine for distance communication.

1876   Alexander Graham Bell demonstrates his voice telephone at the Centennial Exhibition in Philadelphia.

1893   Elisha Gray's Telautograph, an electric writing machine for use with the telephone, is demonstrated at the World's Fair in Chicago.

1920s Bell Telephone Laboratories established.

Bell System creates the "Deaf Set" for hard of hearing persons.

Bell System demonstrates transmission of pictures over telephone lines.

1934   Congress passes the Communications Act, which includes a provision requiring the recently established Federal Communications Commission (FCC) to ensure universal services as far as possible to all the people of the United States.

1957   Bell Laboratories demonstrates a TV-Telephone.

1964   The first long-distance call by a deaf person using electric writing machines occurs.

Robert H. Weitbrecht, a Deaf physicist, develops an acoustic telephone coupler for use with teletypewriters (TTY) by deaf people.

First public demonstration of a TTY call between deaf persons takes place in a hotel at the Alexander Graham Bell Association for the Deaf and Hard of Hearing convention in Salt Lake City, Utah.

AT&T demonstrates the Picturephone at the World's Fair in New York City.

1966   Andrew Saks establishes the first telephone relay service in Redwood City, California.

James C. Marsters establishes the second telephone relay service in Pasadena, California.

Robert H. Weitbrecht files a patent for the "Frequency-Shift Teletypewriter."

Number of TTYs in use: 18.

1968 AT&T reaches an agreement with the Alexander Graham Bell Association for the Deaf and Hard of Hearing to distribute TTYs.

Teletypewriters for the Deaf Distribution Committee (TDDC) is established by the National Association of the Deaf and the Alexander Graham Bell Association for the Deaf and Hard of Hearing.

Number of TTYs in use: 174.

1970 Weitbrecht's patent for the modem is approved by the U.S. Patent Office.

FCC permits connection of devices not provided by the telephone company to the telephone network.

Number of TTYs in use: 900.

1971 TTYs are installed in police departments in Dallas and Los Angeles, the first efforts to provide emergency assistance to deaf people.

1972 Microminiaturization of electronic circuits leads to lighter and quieter devices manufactured by HAL Communications Corporation and MAGSAT.

Number of TTYs in use: 2,500.

1973 The Rehabilitation Act is signed by President Richard Nixon.

1975 The first statewide, toll-free relay service is established in North Dakota.

1976 Number of TTYs in use: 20,000.

1980 AT&T establishes toll-free TTY operator service.

California begins free TTY distribution program for deaf residents.

1982 Congress passes the Telecommunications Act of 1982; the law expands telephone access for people with disabilities, based on the universal service obligation.

Number of TTYs in use: 180,000.

1985 More states provide TTY distribution programs.

1990 President George Bush signs the Americans With Disabilities Act (ADA) of 1990.

Advances in fiberoptic technology improve research developments in video telephones.

1991 Federal relay standards are defined by Title IV of the ADA.

1995 Sprint experiments with video relay interpreting in Texas.

1996 President Bill Clinton signs the Telecommunications Reform Act of 1996, directing the FCC and a joint board of state and federal communications regulators to reexamine the concept of universal service.

2003 Sorenson Media distributes the VP-100 to deaf people at no cost.

2007 The Registry of Interpreters for the Deaf (RID) publishes Video Relay Service Standard Practice Paper.

Appendix B

Methods and Procedure

GROUNDED THEORY

This study aimed to explore the shared experiences of interpreters working in a video relay service (VRS) environment without the interference of preconceived notions regarding the work. Toward this aim, grounded theory, a systematic research method used primarily in the social sciences, was employed. The goal of grounded theory is to develop an explanatory theory rather than verify an existing theory (Glaser & Strauss, 1967). To examine the decision making of interpreters in their daily work in VRS, this study used the following elements of grounded theory: (a) transcription, (b) coding, (c) constant comparative method, and (d) categorization. Grounded theory methods presuppose that there is no simple explanation for people's actions given that everyday situations are complex; rather, in grounded theory, it is important to gather "multiple perspectives on events and build variation into our analytic schemes" (Corbin & Strauss, 2008, p. 8). Using grounded theory as a framework, I interviewed 20 VRS interpreters who work between American Sign Language (ASL) and English, focusing on their experiences with the constraints placed on their work in the VRS setting.

Participants were initially recruited via an email distributed through the Registry of Interpreters for the Deaf (RID) Video Interpreters Members Section (VIMS) member listserv (see Appendix C). Following grounded theory methods, the constant comparative method was used to assess data and recruit further participants. In an effort to include a variety of perspectives, participants were asked to recommend additional participants who have had a different experience than their own and who may be willing to take part in the research.

INTERVIEWS

The method of conducting interviews is especially appropriate when investigative sites are inaccessible to the researcher. Outside observation is often prohibited in VRS call centers due to regulation of call confidentiality (Telecommunications Relay Service Rules, 2011). Unable to observe interpreters in the VRS setting, I conducted in-depth interviews with 20 interpreters to investigate their experiences and perceptions of their work in the VRS setting. Using interview data, I analyzed interpreter perceptions of the efficacy of their work in light of the various constraints established by the Federal Communications Commission (FCC) and corporate VRS providers. In addition, I documented how VRS interpreters exercised professional autonomy in relation to the organizational constraints in their workplace.

To elicit responses without influencing or leading the conversation, interviews were conducted as guided discussions rather than adhering to a strict interview protocol (Taylor & Bogdan, 1998). A highly structured interview may lead participants to believe that there is a right or wrong answer to interview questions, possibly influencing their responses. To avoid influencing the discussion, I began each interview with a casual opening conversation as a means of building initial rapport with the participant. For example, during one interview, I asked a participant how she was enjoying her summer and we spoke briefly about our respective summer plans. In another interview, we briefly commiserated about our struggle with Skype connectivity that morning. As recommended by Spradley (1979), I then provided a general project overview to the participants. To ensure that each participant was given the same information, I followed a script regarding the project overview (see Appendix D). I then asked the following open-ended question: Tell me about a *typical* VRS call. When the discussion seemed to be at a point of closing, I added the second question: Tell me about an *atypical* VRS call. Although these were the only two scripted questions used in this study, the initial project overview script (which was read to each participant) informed the participants of the goal of my study: "Thank you for your participation in this research study on interpreters' decision making in their work in video relay service settings." In addition, each participant signed an Institutional Review Board (IRB) consent form prior to the interview. The consent form included the title of my study. This may have also alerted the participants to the goal of the study.

I followed the same interview protocol for each participant but also included unscripted probe questions based on the participants' responses to the two protocol questions. The initial questions served as starting points for conversation rather than an attempt to constrain interpreters to these topics. Additional questions were asked throughout the course of the interviews. For example, when one participant began to discuss the varying temperaments of deaf callers, I asked her to describe an instance in which the caller was particularly emotional. Similarly, when a participant mentioned the stress she felt with certain VRS calls, I asked for her to describe her most recent 911 call.

An assumption in grounded theory, as described by Taylor and Bogdan (1998), is that what participants "say to interviewers will depend on how they view the interviewers and how they think the interviewers view them" (p. 98). As a result, participants may be inclined to respond in a way that they think will satisfy the interviewer. Participants may also suppress information if they feel the interviewer may view their actions as wrong. As discussed by Taylor and Bogdan (1998), "Interviews are subject to the same fabrications, deceptions, exaggerations, and distortions that characterize other conversations between persons" (p. 98). Hypothetically, an interpreter who wants to appear competent in the eyes of the interviewer may not volunteer that she recently transferred a call between a pregnant woman and her doctor after 2 minutes because she was unfamiliar with the medical vocabulary or uncomfortable with the topic being discussed. In an effort to minimize the feeling of uneasiness with expressing their experience, I consciously used language that was inviting and friendly. For example, I often empathized with the challenging experiences of participants and expressed interest in their stories, encouraging them to tell me more.

In an effort to maintain a relaxed conversational style, I incorporated some of Spradley's (1979) 10 characteristics of friendly conversation, including (a) greetings, (b) lack of explicit purpose, (c) avoiding repetition, (d) asking questions, (e) expressing interest, (f) expressing ignorance, (g) taking turns, (h) abbreviating, (i) pausing, and (j) leave taking (pp. 56–58). I consciously used the features of friendly conversation in the discourse, except for lack of explicit purpose because the initial script read to each participant included the general topic of the study.

In interviews conducted using grounded theory methods, interviewers strive to remain nonjudgmental and conduct interviews in a relaxed and conversational manner. Interviews take place in comfortable environments, and participants are encouraged to provide narratives about their experiences. In this study, interviews were conducted using video conferencing software (Skype or FaceTime). The participants were often at home, dressed casually, and eating a meal or drinking a cup of coffee. The conversational nature used in this study was deliberately created with the goal of generating interest in the participants, which allowed me to probe for richer details in the responses.

PARTICIPANTS

Participant selection was conducted in adherence with grounded theory methods for theoretical sampling. In this approach, sample size is determined toward the end of a research study as opposed to at the beginning (Taylor & Bogdan, 1998). Theoretical sampling uses theories emerging from data to guide participant selection. In this way, the researcher is led to seek variation in participant experience or to investigate an emerging category more thoroughly (Coyne, 1997). For example, after eight interviews with female video interpreters, I sought male interpreters to ensure that variation in interpreter experience was represented. As I continued data collection, I incorporated three male interpreters into the study. Consistent data analysis supported further participant selection to further investigate topics (Corbin & Strauss, 2008).

The initial participants were selected in the following manner. First, I contacted the RID VIMS with the request for distribution of a recruitment email (see Appendix C) via their listserv. VIMS members either work as video relay and video remote interpreters or are interested in video interpreting work. Through the VIMS structure, members are able to share information and discuss common interests pertaining to their work. VIMS members are located across the United States and represent different age groups, thus allowing for the investigation of diverse interpreter participants. To ensure that I was successfully including diverse perspectives, a list of survey respondents was compiled in an Excel spreadsheet noting the following information: (a) state of residence, (b) age, (c) number of VRS providers they had worked for, (d) names of VRS providers they had worked for, (e) number of years worked as a video interpreter, (f) positions held for a VRS provider (e.g., manager, CA), (g) interpreter certification held, (h) number of hours per week working in VRS, and (i) additional notes. Most participants did not have concerns regarding sharing this information; however, in some instances, the participant preferred not to disclose this information via email and only provided this information when we met for the interview.

Interviews were conducted from November 2013 to November 2014, at which point I determined that I had achieved "theoretical" saturation in my data collection. Saturation is defined as "the point in research when all concepts are well defined and explained" (Corbin & Strauss, 2008, p. 145). Charmaz (2006) stated that saturation does not refer to repetition of information, but rather to the point in which no new information or emerging patterns can be found by continuing to interview further participants. I determined that no new information or patterns were found in the responses after interviewing 20 participants, so I concluded the interviewing process.

Participants in this study lived and worked in 14 different states throughout the United States. The mean age of participants was 39.5 years old, with a range of 26 to 59 years of age. Participants reported working in the VRS setting between 6 months and 12 years, with a mean of 6.3 years of VRS experience. The participants worked in VRS between 5 and 40 hours per week. Although the majority of communications assistants (CAs) in the United States work for a single VRS provider that holds 90% of the VRS market, I did not control for this factor. Participants reported professional work experience with four different VRS providers. Some interpreters worked with several different providers over the span of their VRS interpreting career and discussed their experiences with each provider.

All participants were certified; 19 held RID national certification and 1 held BEI[1] certification. Although VRS providers also employ noncertified interpreters, certain providers require national certification prior to hiring; therefore, it may be that certified interpreters were more comfortable participating in a research study about VRS.

MATERIALS AND TASKS

Prior to their scheduled interview appointment, participants completed a consent form approved by the IRB and a video release form. Participants

---

1. BEI stands for the Board for Evaluation of Interpreters, the governing body responsible for the testing and certifying of signed language interpreters in Texas.

received compensation of a $20 Visa gift card for their involvement in the study. Each of the participants lived at a distance from where I was based; therefore, the gift cards were mailed to the preferred mailing address of each participant at the conclusion of the interview.

As described earlier, each interview began with a description the procedures and goals of the study in English (Appendix D). To ensure anonymity of the participants, each individual was asked to create a pseudonym to serve as an identifier in future presentations and publications associated with this research. All documents were subsequently labeled using the chosen pseudonym of each participant.

Interviews were conducted using video meeting software such as FaceTime or Skype. Communication occurred primarily in spoken English; however, participants switched to ASL for varying reasons throughout the interview (e.g., to reference communication from a deaf caller). To capture these moments, the meetings were recorded using iShowU HD Pro software (version 2.3.2, 2012), which captures and saves video for later viewing. Due to video recording of interviews, an anonymous analysis could not be conducted; however, after transcription, interviews were identified using the participant's chosen pseudonym. Participants were informed that I might contact them again to pursue further information, and all agreed to follow-up contact. After each interview, I compiled a verbatim transcription of the entire conversation and gave each participant the opportunity to review the written transcript of the interview; no participants expressed interest in reviewing the transcript.

ANALYSIS

In this study, I conducted both within-subject and between-subject comparisons. The within-subject analysis focused on the identification of major themes expressed by a single participant in reference to their use of professional autonomy in VRS settings. In the between-subject comparisons, I compared the similarities and differences between the themes expressed by the entire group of interpreters who were interviewed. Quotes exhibiting decisions made by interpreters were collected to illustrate the thematic analysis.

I analyzed interview data using the constant comparative method, an approach associated with grounded theory (Charmaz, 2001; see also Emerson, Fretz, & Shaw, 2011; Glaser & Strauss, 1967; Taylor & Bogdan,

1998). In this method, data analysis immediately follows data collection. Data analysis occurs in the form of postinterview data transcription, line-by-line coding of identified themes, and comparison of themes discovered within data. Themes are identified either directly from language used by the participants (e.g., shared vocabulary, similar actions, patterns in ideas) or are assigned by the researcher in reference to the participant's meaning in the data obtained (e.g., common topics, similar feelings). The identification of themes fosters the researcher's ability to pursue further information from future participants.

After each interview, I uploaded video data into ELAN software (version 4.9.1-b, 2013) on my personal laptop. ELAN is designed for the annotation and analysis of video/audio data via an interface that aligns data with categories (tiers) created by the researcher. To preserve participant confidentiality, all video and ELAN data files were labeled using the participant's chosen pseudonym and saved on an external hard drive, which was kept in a secure location at my home.

I created a complete transcription of each participant's comments under one tier in the ELAN system, as well as developed a complete transcription of my own questions or comments in a separate tier. An advantage of ELAN is that the tiers can be exported into Microsoft Word, which allowed me to view the data in a dialogue format. Themes within the interviews were then identified to reflect the actions and experience of interpreters in regard to their work in VRS settings (e.g., autonomy, training, resistance). Consistent with grounded theory, after reviewing the interviews, a codebook of themes was created using an Excel spreadsheet in order to track emerging themes. During the data coding process, specific quotes regarding the use of professional autonomy were noted within the codebook.

After emerging themes were identified using a within-subject analysis, an across-subject analysis was conducted by revisiting prior coded transcripts comparing identified themes with the newly emerging themes. Throughout the analysis process, I selected various participant quotes, which I incorporated into the codebook; this technique supplemented my investigation of patterns or relationships across cases. Once all data were collected, transcribed, and coded, I then sorted the themes into color-coded categories and counted the frequency of the emergence of each theme.

The role of the researcher using grounded theory principles is to "understand and represent the meaning of some type of behavior or phenomenon. To do this more effectively, an effort is made to make this 'formulation' within a 'naïve attitude' in which biases, expectations, and hypotheses are put aside" (Lopez, 1999, p. 38). During the development of this study, I identified my potential biases from my experience of working in the VRS setting. In addition, after my initial data analysis, I sought the assistance of two supplemental reviewers to ensure my perception of data did not reflect any bias.

I selected two independent reviewers to examine a sample of data using the same methods of thematic analysis. Both reviewers were active members of my local interpreting community, had conducted research on interpreting, and were teaching in the interpreter education program where I am employed. At the time of the review, both of the reviewers had worked in VRS for over 10 years and were still employed by VRS companies.

Using a random number generator, five interview transcriptions were selected for the external reviewers to assess. From the selected transcripts, I chose five quotes that contained comments about professional autonomy. I shared these quotes with the reviewers and asked them to identify themes within the narratives. I first read a script to the reviewers that explained the goal of the study, provided the definition of a theme, and described the process for theme identification. The reviewers were given two practice trials (two participants, five quotes each) on the task of theme identification. The reviewers and I then discussed the process and compared the themes they identified in the practice trial. The reviewers then proceeded with identifying themes for three additional participant selections (5 quotes each, for a total of 15 quotes). As a group, the reviewers and I then discussed the themes they had identified within the texts.

Following the review session, I coded data for themes identified by the external reviewers and determined whether they matched my own analysis. I rated the themes as a "match" when the reviewers and I (a) used the exact same word to describe the theme, or (b) used synonyms that expressed the same thematic idea. I coded items with one of three numerical designations:

- 1: All three people (i.e., myself and the two reviewers) identified the same theme within a selection of the interview transcription.
- 0.5: Only one of the reviewers identified the same theme that I had identified.
- 0: Neither of the reviewers identified the same theme that I had identified.

Data analysis was corroborated by the reviewers' analysis at a 93% match rate (14 of the 15 items were coded as a match). In two instances, only one reviewer identified the same theme that I identified in the data.

Appendix C

Interview Script

To ensure that all of the participants receive the exact same information, I need to read from this script, okay?

First, thank you for your participation in this research study on interpreters' decision making in their work in video relay service settings. Before we begin the interview, I want to ask if you have any questions about any of the forms that you recently filled out.

Today we will be talking about your experience working in VRS. I want you to know that our conversation today will be kept entirely confidential.

This interview takes approximately 1 hour. If you feel you need a break at any time, please let me know. Ready to begin?

Great! Let's begin.

Appendix D

Additional Questions Posed by Interviewer

As discussed in Appendix B, "Methods and Procedure," not all participants were asked all of the questions. In some instances, participants raised an issue without a prompt. In others, the discussion was not raised due to prior comments from the participant either directing the conversation toward or away from the question (e.g., "You mentioned that you used to work more hours. Why did you reduce the number of hours that you work per week?" or "You mentioned that you worked for two companies. What made you switch from one company to another?").

Do you sign in to the computer itself, or do you have to check in to show that you are there?

You mentioned ergonomics. What types of things do you do for the goal of ergonomics?

How many people usually work in the center at the same time?

What time does the last person leave the center?

What types of calls do you tend to get during a daytime shift? What about night shifts?

Can you tell me about the last time that you called for a team? If you had already called for a team, would that impact your decision to call for a team later in the day?

You mentioned you worked for two companies. What made you switch from one company to the other?

You mentioned that there is a difference in what you do when you interpret in the community as compared to when you work in VRS. What's the difference? Can you give me an example?

Why did you decide to work night shifts? Why did you decide to work day shifts?

You mentioned boundaries. Can you tell me about the last time you feel you stepped over your boundaries as an interpreter?

You mentioned that it is "call after call after call." Have you done anything to support yourself in the work?

Do you make decisions differently at night than you would during the day? Why?

You mentioned that the provider judges your performance. What do they do?

What does that mean—performance-based scheduling?

Do you see your stats often? How are they communicated to you? Do your stats impact your decisions?

You mentioned that calls are often pixelated and blurry. Do you do anything differently with those calls to compensate for that?

You mentioned your personal ethics. Can you give me an example of the last time you used your personal ethics during a call?

You mentioned transferring a call. Can you tell me about the last time that you transferred a call?

You mentioned the caller complained. Who did they complain to? What was the result of that complaint?

You mentioned that you didn't have control. Can you tell me more about the types of situations you feel you can't control in VRS?

Can you tell me about how you typically take breaks during your shift?

You mentioned being an ally to the deaf community. Can you tell me about the last time you acted as an ally?

You mentioned that you used to work more hours. Why did you reduce the number of hours you work per week?

Can you tell me about your last emergency call? Did you do anything differently during that call because you felt it was an emergency?

Can you tell me about your last 911 call? Did you do anything differently during the call because it was 911? Did you do anything after that call?

Does the provider keep track of how often you call for a team?

You said that you typically follow the rules. What is an example of a rule that you follow? Is there a rule that you do not follow?

You mentioned that it is difficult to interpret for callers when they are too far away from the screen, eating, or laying down. Do you do anything differently with those calls? Can you tell me about the last time that happened?

You mentioned that you have to work 12 hours during the course of 3 months. What happens if you don't?

You mentioned you prefer not to work nights. Why?

How do you request a team?

What are the repercussions if someone notices that you transferred a call outside the center?

Can you tell me about the last call you had where the caller was angry with you? What do you do differently during the call when you feel that the caller is angry/abusive? Do you do anything after the call?

What do you do if you call for a team and you feel that they are not an appropriate support for the call?

You mentioned that you shared visual information. What kind of visual information did you share?

What are the repercussions for calling a team too often?

Can you tell me about the last call that you felt was particularly emotional? Did you do anything differently for that call? What did you do after the call?

Can you tell me about your schedule? How do you set up your shifts?

You mentioned that you use instant messaging to communicate with other interpreters. Can you tell me about the last time that you used it?

You mentioned that you felt you educated the deaf caller. How so? Why did you make that decision?

In what other situations do you feel you need to "give the power to the deaf person"?

Did you report that caller? How did you report the caller? Did anything result from your having reported the caller?

You mentioned that you have to keep a call for 10 minutes. Do you always do that? When have you not done that?

You mentioned a caller who had a physical disability. Do you do anything differently with those calls?

You mentioned that you called a specific team. Why? How?

Can you tell me about the last time you were told not to announce that there was an interpreter on the line? What did you do differently?

Why do you think they asked for a male interpreter? Did you do anything differently because they asked for a male interpreter?

You mentioned that you stayed late after your shift ended. What led you to make that decision?

Can you tell me about your last call that was a phone tree?

References

Abbott, A. (1988). *The system of professions: An essay on the division of expert labor*. Chicago, IL: University of Chicago Press.

Adam, R., Carty, B., & Stone, C. (2011). Ghostwriting: Deaf translators within the Deaf community. *Babel Revue Internationale De La Traduction/ International Journal of Translation Babel, 57*(4), 375–393.

Alley, E. (2014). "Who makes the rules anyway?": Reality and perception of guidelines in video relay service interpreting. *The Interpreters' Newsletter, 19*, 13–26.

Americans With Disabilities Act of 1990, Pub. L. No. 101–336, Section 225 (1990).

Bailey, J. (2005). VRS: The ripple effect of supply and demand. *RID VIEWS, 22*(3), 15.

Ball, C. (2013). *Legacies and legends: History of interpreter education from 1800 to the 21st century*. Edmonton, Canada: Interpreting Consolidated.

Ball, C. (2007). *The history of American Sign Language Interpreting education*. (Unpublished doctoral diss.) Capella University. Minneapolis, MN ProQuest Dissertations and Theses.

Board of Education of Hendrick Hudson Central School District v. Amy Rowley, 458 U.S. 176 (1982). Retrieved from https://www.wrightslaw.com/ law/caselaw/ussupct.rowley.htm

Bocian, B. (2012). *Grabbing the VRS bull by the horns, is it possible? An investigation of video relay service demands and controls*. Unpublished manuscript, Department of Interpretation, Gallaudet University, Washington, DC.

Bolton, S., & Houlihan, M. (2005). The (mis)representation of customer service. *Work Employment & Society, 19*(4), 685–703. Retrieved from http://wes .sagepub.com.pearl.stkate.edu/content/19/4/685.full.pdf.html

Bower, K. (2013). Stress and burnout in video relay service interpreting. *RID VIEWS, 30*(3), 18–19.

Brasel, B., Montanelli, D., & Quigley, S. (1974). The component skills of interpreting as viewed by interpreters. *Journal of Rehabilitation of the Deaf, 7*(3), 20–27.

Braverman, H. (1998). *Labor and monopoly capital: The degradation of work in the twentieth century*. New York, NY: Monthly Review Press.

Brophy, E. (2011). Language put to work: Cognitive capitalism, call center labor, and worker inquiry. *Journal of Communication Inquiry, 35*(4), 410–416.

Brunson, J. (2006). Commentary on the professional status of sign language interpreters: An alternative perspective. *Journal of Interpretation,* 1–10.

Brunson, J. (2010). Visually experiencing a phone call: The calculated consumer labor deaf people perform to gain access through video relay service. *Disability Studies Quarterly, 30*(2). Retrieved from http://dsq-sds.org/article/view/1245/1273#endnoteref01

Brunson, J. (2011). *Video relay service interpreters*. Washington, DC: Gallaudet University Press.

Brunson, J. (2018). The irrational component in the rational system: Interpreters talk about their motivation to work in video relay service. In J. Napier, R. Skinner, & S. Braun (Eds.), *Here or there: Research on interpreting via video link* (pp. 36–60). Washington, DC: Gallaudet University Press.

Carr-Saunders, A., & Wilson, P. (1933). *The professions*. Oxford, United Kingdom: The Clarendon Press.

Carter, S., & Lauritsen, R. (1974). Interpreter recruitment, selection and training. *Journal of Rehabilitation of the Deaf, 7*(3), 52–62.

Chandler, D. (n.d.). *Technological or media determinism*. Retrieved from http://eldar.cz/mishutka/mn/%C2%9Akola/technologie/Technological%20or%20Media%20Determinism.doc

Charbotel, B., Croidieu, S., Vohito, M., Guerin, A., Renaud, L., Jaussaud, J., & Bergeret, A. (2008). Working conditions in call-centers, the impact on employee health: A transversal study. Part II. *International Archives of Occupational and Environmental Health, 82*(6), 747–756.

Charmaz, K. (2001). Grounded theory. In R. Emerson (Ed.), *Contemporary field research* (2nd ed.). Prospect Heights, IL: Waveland Press.

Charmaz, K. (2006). *Constructing grounded theory: A practical guide through qualitative analysis*. London, United Kingdom: SAGE Publications, Inc.

Cokely, D. (1992). *Interpretation: A sociologinguistic model*. Burtonsville, MD: Linstock Press.

Cokely, D. (2005). Shifting positionality: A critical examination of the turning point in the relationship of interpreters and the deaf community. In M. Marschark, R. Peterson, & E. A. Winston (Eds.), *Sign language interpreting and interpreter education: Directions for research and practice* (pp. 3–28). New York, NY: Oxford University Press.

Commission on Collegiate Interpreter Education (CCIE). (2015). Mission. Retrieved from http://ccie-accreditation.org

Communications Act, 47 U.S.C. 151–160 (1934, as amended by the telecommunications act of 1996). Retrieved from transition.fcc.gov/Reports/1934new.pdf

Corbin, J., & Strauss, A. (2008). *Basics of qualitative research: Techniques and procedures for developing grounded theory* (3rd ed.). Los Angeles, CA: SAGE Publications, Inc.

Cowan, R. S. (1976). The "Industrial Revolution" in the home: Household technology and social change in the 20th century. *Technology and Culture, 17*(1), 1–23.

Cox, G. B. (2003). *The interpretation factor: Overcoming the language barrier at the trial of the major war criminals before the international military tribunal at Nuremberg.* (Unpublished master's thesis), University of Houston, Texas.

Coyne, I. T. (1997). Sampling in qualitative research. Purposeful and theoretical sampling; merging or clear boundaries? *Journal of Advanced Nursing, 26,* 623–630.

Davies, C. (1983). Professionals in bureaucracies: The conflict thesis revisited. In R. Dingwall & P. Lewis (Eds.), *The sociology of the professions: Lawyers, doctors, and others* (pp. 177–194). London, United Kingdom: Macmillan.

Dean, R., & Pollard, R. (2001). Application of demand-control theory to sign language interpreting: Implications for stress and interpreter training. *Journal of Deaf Studies and Deaf Education, 6*(1), 1–14.

Dorros, I. (1969). Picturephone. *Bell Laboratories Record, 47*(5), 136–141.

Education for All Handicapped Children Act of 1975. Pub. L. No. 94–142, 89 Stat. 773. (1975). Retrieved from http://www.gpo.gov/fdsys/pkg/STATUTE-89/pdf/STATUTE-89-Pg773.pdf

ELAN [computer software]. (2013). Retrieved from https://tla.mpi.nl/tools/tla-tools/elan/

Emerson, R. M., Fretz, R. I., & Shaw, L. L. (2011). *Writing ethnographic fieldnotes* (2nd ed.). Chicago, IL: The University of Chicago Press.

Evetts, J. (2006). Introduction: Trust and professionalism: Challenges and occupational changes. *Current Sociology, 54*(4), 515–531.

Fant, L. J. (1974). The California State University-Northridge approach to training interpreters. *Journal of Rehabilitation of the Deaf, 7*(3), 44–46.

Fant, L. (1990). *Silver threads: A personal look at the first twenty-five years of the Registry of Interpreters for the Deaf.* Silver Spring, MD: RID Publications.

Federal Communications Commission. (n.d.). Video relay service: FCC consumer facts. Retrieved from http://www.fcc.gov/guides/video-relay-services

Federal Communications Commission. (2011). Report and order and further notice of proposed rulemaking: Structure and practices of the video relay service program (FCC 11–54).

Flynn, S. V. (2009). *A grounded theory of the altruism and self-interest phenomenon within the counseling profession.* (Unpublished doctoral diss.), University of Northern Colorado, Greeley.

Forestal, E. M. (2011). *Deaf interpreters: Exploring their processes of interpreting* (Unpublished doctoral dissertation). Capella University, Minneapolis, MN.

Freidson, E. (1983). The theory of professions: State of the art. In R. Dingwall & P. Lewis (Eds.), *The sociology of the professions: Lawyers, doctors, and others* (pp. 19–37). London, United Kingdom: Macmillan.

Gaiba, F. (1998). *The origins of simultaneous interpretation: The Nuremberg trial.* Ottawa, Canada: University of Ottawa Press.

Glaser, B., & Strauss, A. (1967). *The discovery of grounded theory.* Hawthorne, NY: Aldine.

Goode, W. (1957). Community within a community: The professions. *American Sociological Review, 22*(2), 194–200.

Greenwood, E. (1957). Attributes of a profession. *Social Work, 2*(3), 45–55.

Grint, K. (2005). *The sociology of work: An introduction* (3rd ed.). Cambridge, United Kingdom: Polity Press.

Gustafsson, K., Norström, E., & Fioretos, I. (2013). The interpreter: A cultural broker? In C. Schäffner, K. Kredens, & Y. Fowler (Eds.), *Interpreting in a changing landscape: Selected papers from critical link 6* (pp. 187–202). Amsterdam, The Netherlands: John Benjamins Publishing.

Gustason, G. (1985). Interpreters entering public school employment. *American Annals of the Deaf, 130*, 265–266.

Hochschild, A. (1983). *The managed heart.* Berkeley, CA: University of California Press.

Hoza, J. (2010). *Team interpreting as collaboration and interdependence.* Alexandria, VA: Registry of Interpreters for the Deaf.

Hsieh, E. (2014). Emerging trends and the corresponding challenges in bilingual health communication. In B. Nicodemus & M. Metzger (Eds.), *Investigations in healthcare interpreting* (pp. 70–103). Washington, DC: Gallaudet University Press.

IDEAL Group. (2012). *Steve Jacobs and the history of video relay service in the United States.* Retrieved from http://www.ideal-group.org

Ingram, R. (1974). A communication model of the interpreting process. *Journal of Rehabilitation of the Deaf, 7*(3), 3–8.

iShowU HD Pro [computer software]. (2012). Retrieved from https://www.shinywhitebox.com/ishowuhd

Johnson, L., Taylor, M., & Witter-Merithew, A. (2005). *Video relay services interpreting task analysis report.* https://www.unco.edu/cebs/asl-interpreting/pdf/library/vrs-task-analysis-report.pdf

Karasek, R. (1979). Job demands, job decision latitudes, and mental strain: Implications for job design. *Administrative Science Quarterly, 24*, 285–307.

Kasher, A. (2005). Professional ethics and collective professional autonomy: A conceptual analysis. *Journal of European Ethics Network, 11*(1), 67–98.

Keating, E., & Mirus, G. (2003). American Sign Language in virtual space: Interactions between deaf users of computer-mediated video communication and the impact of technology on language practices. *Language in Society, 32*, 693–714.

Kelly, J. (2001). *Transliteration: Show me the English.* Alexandria, VA: RID Press.

Krause, E. A. (1996). *Death of the guilds: Professions, states, and the advance of capitalism, 1930 to the present*. New Haven, CT: Yale University Press.

Lang, H. G. (2000). *A phone of our own: The deaf insurrection against Ma Bell*. Washington, DC: Gallaudet University Press.

Larson, M. (1980). Proletarianization and educated labor. *Theory and Society, 9*(1), 131–175.

Liljegren, A. (2012). Key metaphors in the sociology of professions: Occupations as hierarchies and landscapes. *Comparative Sociology, 11*, 88–112.

Llewellyn-Jones, P., & Lee, R. (2013). Getting to the core of role: Defining interpreters' role-space. *International Journal of Interpreter Education, 5*(2), 54–72.

Lopez, V. A. (1999). *Adolescent male offenders' cognitions and emotions: A grounded theory study of delinquent crime contexts*. (Doctoral diss.) University of Texas at Austin. (Order No. 9956883). Available from ProQuest Dissertations & Theses Global. (304529212).

Macdonald, K. (1995). *The sociology of the professions*. London, United Kingdom: SAGE Publications Inc.

Major, G. C. (2013). *Healthcare interpreting as a relational practice* (Doctoral diss.). Macquarie University, Sydney, Australia.

Marks, A. (2015). Investigating footing shifts in video relay service interpreted interaction. In B. Nicodemus & K. Cagle (Eds.) *Selected papers from the International Symposium on Signed Language Interpretation and Translation Research (Vol. 1)* (pp. 71–96). Washington, DC: Gallaudet University Press.

Martí-Audí, N., Valverde, M., & Heraty, N. (2013). Human resource management in the Spanish call centre sector: The bird cage model of call centre work. *The International Journal of Human Resource Management, 24*(2), 308–329.

Marx, K. (1867/1976). *Capital: Volume 1*. London, United Kingdom: Penguin Books.

Mathers, C. M. (1999). Preparation: More than just a good idea. *RID VIEWS, 16*(8), 1, 5–8.

Meadows, D. H. (2008). *Thinking in systems: A primer*. White River Junction, VT: Chelsea Green Publishing.

Mercer, D. (2006). *Telephone: The life story of a technology*. Westport, CT: Greenwood Press.

Metzger, M. (1999). *Sign language interpreting: Deconstructing the myth of neutrality*. Washington, DC: Gallaudet University Press.

Metzger, M. (2006). Salient studies of signed language interpreting in the context of community interpreting scholarship. *Linguistica Antverpiensia, 5*, 263–291.

Michigan Department of Civil Rights. (2002). *TTY or TDD: The text telephone*. Retrieved from http://www.michdhh.org/assistive_devices/text_telephone.html

Morrison, K. (2006). *Marx, Durkheim, Weber: Formations of modern social thought* (2nd ed.). London, United Kingdom: SAGE Publications, Inc.

Moser-Mercer, B. (2003, Summer). *Remote interpreting: Assessment of human factors and performance parameters.* Retrieved from htttp://www.aiic.net /page1125/remote-interpreting-assessment-of-human-factors-and -performance-parameters/lang

Napier, J. (2011). Signed language interpreting. In K. Malmkjær & K. Windle (Eds.), *The Oxford handbook of translation studies.* Oxford, United Kingdom: Oxford University Press.

National Consortium of Interpreter Education Centers (NCIEC). (2010). *Steps toward identifying effective practices in VRS interpreting.* Retrieved from http://www.interpretereducation.org

Nelson, R. A. (1963). *History of teletypewriter development.* Retrieved from http://www.rtty.com/history/nelson.htm

No Child Left Behind Act of 2001, Pub. L. No. 107–110, § 115, Stat. 1425 (2002).

Nowell, R., & Stuckless, R. (1974). An interpreter training program. *Journal of Rehabilitation of the Deaf, 7*(3), 69–75.

Oppenheimer, J., Davis, M., Carroll, B., Jr. (Writers), & Asher, W. (Director). (1952, September). Job switching [Television series episode]. In *I love Lucy.* Los Angeles, CA: Desilu Studios.

Padden, C., & Humphries, T. (1988). *Deaf in America: Voices from a culture.* Cambridge, MA: Harvard University Press.

Padden, C., & Humphries, T. (2005). *Inside deaf culture.* Cambridge, MA: Harvard University Press.

Parsons, T. (1939). The professions and social structure. *Social Forces, 17*(4), 457–467.

Peterson, R. (2011). Profession in pentimento: A narrative inquiry into interpreting in video settings. In B. Nicodemus & L. Swabey (Eds.), *Advances in interpreting research: Inquiry in action* (pp. 199–223). Amsterdam, The Netherlands: John Benjamin Publishing.

Pöchhacker, F. (2004). *Introducing interpreting studies.* New York, NY: Routledge.

Postman, N. (1992). *Technopoly: The surrender of culture to technology.* New York, NY: Alfred A. Knopf.

Preston, P. (1994). *Mother father deaf: Living between sound and silence.* Cambridge, MA: Harvard University Press.

Rafaeli, A., Ziklik, L., & Doucet, L. (2008). The impact of call center employees' customer orientation behaviors on service quality. *Journal of Service Research, 10*(3), 239–255.

Registry of Interpreters for the Deaf (RID). (2005). *Code of professional conduct.* Retrieved from http://www.rid.org/ethics/code-of-professional-conduct

Registry of Interpreters for the Deaf (RID). (2007a). *Team interpreting standard practice paper.* Retrieved from https://drive.google.com/file/d/ 0B3DKvZMflFLdVzZpaUtraW5xZG8/view

Registry of Interpreters for the Deaf (RID). (2007b). *Video relay service standard practice paper.* Retrieved from http://rid.org

Registry of Interpreters for the Deaf (RID). (2015a). *Mission.* Retrieved from http://www.rid.org/about-rid/mission-vision-statements/

Registry of Interpreters for the Deaf (RID). (2015b). *Filing an EPS complaint.* Retrieved from http://rid.org/ethics/file-a-complaint/

Registry of Interpreters for the Deaf Video Interpreting Committee. (2008). *Video relay service and video remote interpreting: What's the difference?* Retrieved from http://rid.org

Rehabilitation Act of 1973. (1973). Retrieved from http://www.hhs.gov

Riekehof, L. (1974). Interpreter training at Gallaudet College. *Journal of Rehabilitation of the Deaf, 7*(3), 47–51.

Ritzer, G. (2008). *The McDonaldization of society 5.* Los Angeles, CA: Pine Forge Press.

Roy, C. B. (1993). The problem with definitions, descriptions, and the role metaphors of interpreters. *Journal of Interpretation, 6*(1), 127–154.

Roy, C. B. (2000). *Interpreting as a discourse process.* New York, NY: Oxford University Press.

Roziner, I., & Shlesinger, M. (2010). Much ado about something remote. *Interpreting, 12*(2), 214–247.

Ruboi, A. I., & Martí, I. A. (2013). The role of the interpreter in educational settings: Interpreter, cultural mediator or both? In C. Schäffner, K. Kredens, & Y. Fowler (Eds.), *Interpreting in a changing landscape: Selected papers from critical link 6* (pp. 203–221). Amsterdam, The Netherlands: John Benjamin Publishing.

Rueschemeyer, D. (1983). Professional autonomy and social control of expertise. In R. Dingwall & P. Lewis (Eds.), *The sociology of the professions: Lawyers, doctors, and others.* London, United Kingdom: Macmillan Press.

Sandstrom, R. (2007). The meanings of autonomy for physical therapy. *Physical Therapy, 87*(1), 98–106.

Schein, J. (1974). Personality characteristics associated with interpreter proficiency. *Journal of Rehabilitation of the Deaf, 7*(3), 33–43.

Schneider, M. A. (2006). *The theory primer: A sociological guide.* Lanham, MD: Rowman & Littlefield.

Seleskovitch, D. (1978). *Interpreting for international conferences.* Arlington, VA: Pen and Booth.

Shaw, R. (1996). Preparing yourself to be an effective legal interpreter. *RID VIEWS, 13*(7), 1, 24–25.

Skinner, R., Napier, J., & Braun, S. (2018). Interpreting via video link: Mapping of the field. In J. Napier, R. Skinner, & S. Braun (Eds.), *Here or there: Research on Interpreting via video link* (pp. 11–35). Washington, DC: Gallaudet University Press.

Smith, D. E. (2006). *Institutional ethnography as practice*. Lanham, MD: Rowman & Littlefield.

Smith, M. R., & Marx, L. (1994). Introduction. In M. R. Smith & L. Marx (Eds.), *Does technology drive history? The dilemma of technological determinism* (pp. ix–xv). Cambridge, MA: The MIT Press.

Sorenson Media. (n.d.). Company profile. Retrieved from http://download .sorensonmedia.com/360v2presskit/Sorenson_Media_Company_Profile _0509.pdf

Spradley, J. (1979). *The ethnographic interview*. Belmont, CA: Wadsworth.

Stone, C. (2009). *Toward a deaf translation norm*. Washington, DC: Gallaudet University Press.

Taylor, P., & Bain, P. (1999). "An assembly line in the head": Work and employee relations in the call centre. *Industrial Relations Journal, 30*(2), 101–117.

Taylor, S., & Bogdan, R. (1998). *Introduction to qualitative research methods: A guidebook and resource* (3rd ed.). New York, NY: John Wiley & Sons, Inc.

Telecommunications Relay Services Rules, 47 C.F.R. §64.601– §64.613 (2011). Retrieved from https://www.ecfr.gov/cgi=bin/ text=idx?e=ecfr&sid=46482a47a845158

Telephones come to terms with sign language. (1989). *New Scientist, 23*(1678), 31. Retrieved from http://books.google.ca/books?id=K9un2-yueXcC&pg=PA31

Turkle, S. (2011). *Alone together: Why we expect more from technology and less from each other*. New York, NY: Basic Books.

Twenty-First Century Communications and Video Accessibility Act of 2010. Pub. L. No. 111–260. (2010). Retrieved from http://www.gpo.gov

U.S. Department of Education. (2007). *Archived: A 25 year history of the IDEA*. Retrieved from http://www2.ed.gov/policy/speced/leg/idea/history.html

U.S. Department of Justice. (2009, November 19). *Twenty-six charged in nationwide scheme to defraud the FCC's video relay service program*. Retrieved from http://www.justice.gov/opa/pr/twenty-six-charged-nationwide-scheme-defraud-fcc-s-video-relay-service-program

U.S. Equal Employment Opportunity Commission. (1978). *Amendments to the Rehabilitation Act of 1973*. Retrieved from http://www.eeoc.gov/eeoc/ history/35th/thelaw/rehab_amendments_1978.html

Vocational Rehabilitation Act Amendments of 1965. (1965). Retrieved from http://www.gpo.gov

Volti, R. (2008). *An introduction to the sociology of work and occupations*. Los Angeles, CA: Pine Forge Press.

Wilensky, H. (1964). The professionalization of everyone? *American Journal of Sociology, 70*(2), 137–158.

Witter-Merithew, A. (1986). Claiming our destiny. *RID VIEWS, 12*(5), 3.

Witter-Merithew, A., Johnson, L., & Nicodemus, B. (2010). Relational autonomy and decision latitude of ASL-English interpreters: Implications for interpreter education. In L. Roberson, & S. Shaw (Eds.), *Proceedings of the 18th National Convention of the Conference of Interpreter Trainers* (pp. 49–66). Fremont, CA: Conference of Interpreter Trainers.

Woodward, J. C. (1975). *How you gonna get to heaven if you can't talk with Jesus: The educational establishment vs. the Deaf community.* Paper presented at the Annual Meeting of the Society for Applied Anthropology, Amsterdam, The Netherlands.

Wren, D. A., & Greenwood, R. G. (1999). Business leaders: A historical sketch of Eli Whitney. *Journal of Leadership & Organizational Studies, 6*(1–2), 128–132.

Index

abusive callers, 55–65

accreditation practices of professions, 15

Americans With Disabilities Act (ADA) of 1990, 37, 58

analysis of study data, 109–10

autonomy: definition of, 21, 28; as socially constructed, 40. *See also* professional autonomy

background knowledge and customer service, 80–81

Bell, Alexander Graham, 29

bilingual-bicultural model of interpreting, 22

billable minutes, 27, 43

breaks: consideration of colleagues when taking, 66–68; length of, 52–54; skipping, 45, 80–82

bureaucracy: decision making within, 95–96; professionals and, 4

burnout, 27, 54, 56

calculated consumer labor, 58–59

California State University, Northridge, 12

call centers: customer orientation behaviors in, 76–77; description of, 18–19; as emotional labor, 27–28; interactions with, 76

callers: abusive, 55–65; reporting, 60–61, 62–64; suicidal, 91; working with before connecting calls, 26–27

CAs. *See* communications assistants

Charter of the International Military Tribunal, 8–9

Children of Deaf Adults (CODA), 14n

cognitive capitalism, 18

commiserating with customers, 84–85

Commission on Collegiate Interpreter Education (CCIE), 14–15

communication facilitator model of interpreting, 22

communications assistants (CAs): adherence to expectations by, 43–44; as assembly line workers, 98–99; complaints against, 57–58, 61–62; conditions of work of, 18–20; constraints on, 26–27, 35–42, 96–97; example of role of, vii; FCC and, 24, 37–38; feedback provided to, 34–35; performance evaluation of, 19–20, 35; requirements for, 16–17, 25; rules governing work of, viii–ix, 43–50. *See also* customer service; efficiency reports; expectations of CAs; self-care; tracking of work

complaints against CAs, 57–58, 61–62

conference calls, 69

cultural mediation, 82–87

customer service: angry or abusive callers and, 56–57; choosing specific team for, 77–79; cultural mediation and, 82–87; in decision making, 96, 99; emergency calls and, 88–90; overview of, 41, 76–77; prioritization of, 47; staying late or skipping breaks and, 80–82; switching CAs and, 90–92

data, external review of, 111–12

data analysis, 109–10

deaf consumers, professionalization of interpreting and, 15–16

deaf interpreters, 78

deaf students, educational opportunities for, 11, 12

dehumanizing of work of interpreters, 35

demand-control schema, 24, 25–26

disconnecting calls, 60–61

Distance Opportunities for Interpreter Training Center, 7

educating customers, 82–83, 84

Education for All Handicapped Children Act of 1975, 11

efficiency reports: as management tool, 48–50; stress associated with, 46, 50–51; teaming and, 70–72; uses of, 43–46

emergency calls, dealing with, 88–90

emotional labor, 27–28, 57, 91–92

emotional support, calling team for, 72–74

evaluation, opportunity for, 6. *See also* efficiency reports; performance evaluation of communications assistants

expectations of CAs: adherence to, 43–44; billable minutes, 27, 43; log-ins, 45, 51–52; modeling realistic, 65–69; 10-minute regulation, 46–47

external review of data, 111–12

Federal Communications Commission (FCC): ADA and, 37–38; decision making by, 39; fraudulent claims submitted to, x; as macrosystem, 36–37; reimbursable time requirements of, 27, 43; "speed of answer" requirement of, 67–68; terminology of, 24;

TRS Mandatory Minimum Standards, 38; VRS rules and guidelines of, viii, ix, 7, 16, 36

feedback provided to CAs, 34–35

footing shifts, 23

freelancing by interpreters, 6

functional transactants, 76

Gallaudet University, 11, 12

grounded theory, 104, 111

guild masters, 1–2

Individuals With Disabilities Enabling Advocacy Link (IDEAL) Group, 32–33

interpreter education programs and VRS rules guidelines, viii

interpreters: as autonomous decision makers, 23–24; CAs compared to, viii; as cultural mediators, 82–87; deaf, 78; dehumanizing work of, 35; friends and family members as, 21; models of role of, 22, 23; technology and, 6, 33–35, 95; work of, and "role-space" model, 26. *See also* communications assistants; Registry of Interpreters for the Deaf

interpreting: models of, 22, 23; professionalization of, 15–17; spoken language, 8–9, 10; team, 40–41, 69. *See also* signed language interpreting; video relay service (VRS) interpreting

interviews: methodology for, 105–7; questions for, 113, 114–16

late, staying, 80–82

legal certification, 79

log-in expectations, 45, 51–52

machine/conduit model of interpreting, 22, 23

managers: confiding in about possible complaints, 57, 62; efficiency reports and, 48–50; planning of shifts of, 53

Marx, Karl, 4–5

"McDonaldization of Society," 17

mental labor, characteristics of, 18

microsystems, 36

moral agents, 76

motivation and remote interpreting, 34–35

mythical sovereigns, 76

National Technical Institute for the Deaf, 11–12

911 calls, 69, 88–89

"Not Announce" calls, dealing with, 86–87

Nuremberg Trials, 8–9

participants in study, 107–9

performance evaluation of communications assistants, 19–20, 35. *See also* efficiency reports

performance expectations, modeling realistic, 65–69

phone trees, dealing with, 83–85

Picturephone, 31–32

power, degree of, and professions, 2, 3

professional autonomy: definition of, x, 21; in VRS setting, overview of, 95–99

professionalization of work: political and legal support for, 10–13; professional associations and, 10, 13–14; recognition of need and, 8–9; role of deaf community in, 15–16; training programs and, 9–10, 16–17; VRS interpreting and criteria for, 16–17

professionals: characteristics of, 1; organizational systems of, 4; trust in, 3

professions: aspects of, 1–2; as communities, 2–3; dynamics of, 16. *See also* professionalization of work

protective action and abusive callers, 57, 61–62, 63

r-calls (rest calls), vii, x

reconnecting calls, 88, 89, 92–94

Registry of Interpreters for the Deaf (RID): Code of Professional Conduct, 39, 86; complaints against interpreters and, 57–58; establishment of, 10; mission and influence of, 13–14; Standard Practice Paper, viii, 26–27; on team interpreting, 69; Video Interpreters Members Section (VIMS), ix

Rehabilitation Act of 1973, 11

relational autonomy, 40

relational work, 28

remote interpreting, constraints on, 34–35

reporting callers, 60–61, 62–64

requirements for communications assistants, 16–17, 25

research on interpreting, 22–23

resistance to rules, 44, 46–47

responsibility, as theme in VRS work, viii–ix

rest calls (r-calls), vii, x

RID. *See* Registry of Interpreters for the Deaf

Rowley, Amy, 11n

scam calls, dealing with, 85–86

scheduling: autonomy and, 50–55; award of shifts, 43, 44–46

self-care: scheduling and, 54–55; switching calls and, 74; taking breaks and, 67

shifts, award of, 43, 44–46

signed language interpreting: origins of, 9; training for, 10, 11–13. *See also* communications assistants; interpreters

simultaneous interpretation, 9

skipping breaks, 45, 80–82

social change and technology, 4–8

social interaction, customer service as, 76

Sorenson Communications, 7

Sorenson Media, 33

"speed of answer" requirement, 67–68

spoken language interpreting, 8–9, 10, 22–23

status of occupations, 1, 5

staying late, 80–82

stress of job: abusive callers and, 55–65; efficiency reports associated with, 46, 50–51; schedule and, 55

suicidal callers, 91

supervision, opportunity for, 6

switching CAs and customer service, 47, 57, 58–60, 90–92

systems: definition of, 36; functioning within, 40, 95–96

team, calling for: choosing specific members for customer service, 77–79; regarding potential complaints, 61–62; scheduling shifts and, 54–55

team interpreting, 40–41, 69

technology: availability of CAs for teams and, 77–78, 79; interpreters and, 6, 33–35, 95; social change and, 4–8, 98;

troubleshooting problems with, 92–94

telecommunications: functionally equivalent access to, 65, 70; history of, 28–33, 101–3

telecommunications relay service (TRS) governance, 36–37

Telecommunications Relay Service Rules, 69–70, 74

teletypewriters (TTYs), 29–31

10-minute regulation, 46–47

text relay service, 30

themes of research, 41–42. *See also* customer service; tracking of work

tough skin, need for, 59–60

tracking of work: abusive callers and, 55–65; calling for team, 69–75; efficiency reports, 43–50; modeling realistic performance expectations, 65–69; overview of, 41; professional autonomy and, 74–75; scheduling, 50–55

transferring calls: to other call centers, 73–74; to other CAs, 47, 57, 58–60, 90–92

transliteration, 13n

TRS (telecommunications relay service) governance, 36–37

TTYs (teletypewriters), 29–31

21st Century Communications and Video Accessibility Act of 2010, 37

unity of feeling with colleagues, 64–65

videophone, introduction of, 5–6

video relay service (VRS): history of, 32–33; as industry, 7–8

video relay service (VRS) interpreting: criteria for professionalization and, 16–17; demands of, 25–26. *See also* communications assistants

video relay service (VRS) providers: autonomy of employees of, 17–18, 21, 24–25, 95–99; benefits of working for, 7; capitalist for-profit model of, 20; fraudulent claims submitted by, x; need for employees of, 25; rules and goals of, 36. *See also* efficiency reports; tracking of work

video streaming technology, introduction of, 6–8

visual information, sharing, for emergency calls, 88–90

Vocational Rehabilitation Act Amendments of 1965, 10–11